Performing Science

A companion website to accompany this book is available online at:
http://education.abrahamsbraund.continuumbooks.com

Please type in the URL above and receive your unique password for access to the book's online resources.

If you experience any problems accessing the resources, please contact Continuum at:
info@continuumbooks.com

Also available from Continuum

100 Ideas for Teaching Science, Sharon Archer
How Science Works, James D. Williams
Practical Work in Secondary Science, Ian Abrahams

Performing Science

Teaching Chemistry, Physics and Biology Through Drama

Edited by Ian Abrahams and Martin Braund

continuum

Continuum International Publishing Group

The Tower Building	80 Maiden Lane
11 York Road	Suite 704
London	New York
SE1 7NX	NY 10038

www.continuumbooks.com

British Library Cataloguing-in-Publication Data
A catalogue record for this book is available from the British Library.

ISBN: 978-1-4411-6071-3 (paperback)

Library of Congress Cataloging-in-Publication Data
A catalog record for this book is available from the Library of Congress.

Typeset by Ben Cracknell Studios
Printed and bound in India

Contents

Acknowledgements

We, as authors owe an enormous debt of thanks to the students and teachers who willingly and enthusiastically gave their time to work with us to produce this book. In particular we would like to thank: Helen Darlington at Helsby High School (A Specialist Science College); Jon Hogg at Ryedale School (A Specialist School in Performing Arts and Science); Mike Pringle at Sherburn High School (A Specialist Science College); as well as Dominic Simpson at Eastbury Comprehensive School (A Specialist Maths and Computing College), Barking; Verity Firth and Ben Tabraham at Park High School (A Technology College and Leading Edge School), Stanmore and Danielle English at Portland Place School, London, along with all students at those schools who took part in the activities. Special thanks must also go to all the laboratory technicians who worked so hard to produce the resources that we needed for these activities.

Introduction

Ian Abrahams

The purpose of this book

This book aims to provide secondary science teachers with all the information that they need to start using drama across all three traditional sciences and to provide it in one readily accessible and easy to use book. We hope that in so doing teachers can use this information to inform and, hopefully, further develop their own teaching practice. The style of the book, containing clear step-by-step instructions, aims to combine 'readability' with clear practical guidance on how to use drama in your science lessons.

Background

My own interest in the use of drama in teaching science was aroused late in my school teaching career during a chance discussion with a drama expert at the University of Warwick back in 2003. I remember arguing that I did not believe that using drama could possibly be an effective method of teaching science, while my colleague was just as adamant that it could. The matter might have gone no further had it not been for that colleague's conviction and perseverance and, as a consequence, a few months later I received an invitation to observe the use of drama in the teaching of science at a secondary school that was taking place as part of that colleague's research study. It would be untrue to say that all my reservations disappeared then and there, but what I saw convinced me that the *effective* use of drama could play a very important part in the teaching of science.

While I began to use drama in my own teaching, my personal 'Road to Damascus' event occurred a few years later when I was a guest at another school. During that visit, and while chatting to students in different classes about practical work, I kept hearing about a role play that had been delivered by an AST (Advanced Skills Teacher, expert teacher) in which the students took on the roles of various components in an electrical circuit. Their recollections were so vivid and detailed and it had evidently made such a lasting impression on them that I contacted the teacher concerned and asked if it would be possible to observe this lesson the next time it was taught. On observing that lesson a few months later, any remaining reservations disappeared and I became a frequent user of drama in my own teaching of physics, including sessions that I have included in this book.

While my own teaching began to incorporate more drama – as did that of colleagues in my science department who also began to see its benefits – it would have gone no further had it not been for two further chance encounters. The first of these, in 2008, was with a commissioning editor from Continuum to discuss a book on practical work which strayed into the area of alternative methods for teaching science and, once I had described the use of drama to this end, I was invited to put together a proposal for a book. The final chance meeting, a year later, occurred at the ESERA (European Science Education Research Association) conference in Istanbul in 2009 when Martin Braund and I happened to be sitting one evening discussing science education over a Turkish coffee. It transpired that both of us were passionate about the use of drama in teaching science and over the next few hours of excited discussion the outlines of a book proposal took shape. In essence, as you will see, we decided that we wanted this book to guide secondary science teachers, many of whom we envisaged would be non-drama specialists (and probably as sceptical about its value in teaching science as I had been), in how to start out in, and then further develop, the use of drama within their teaching repertoires.

Over the next few months we put together a team of experts in biology, chemistry and physics education, all of whom were strongly committed to the use of drama in their own subject areas. Also, and we believe equally importantly, we invited two drama education experts to work with us, as well as science teachers from within our respective PGCE partnership schools, who turned out to be just as excited to work on the book as we were.

We decided to produce 15 clearly presented drama sessions for each of the three traditional science disciplines; with a roughly equal split between those designed for students aged 11–14 and those aged 14–16. The sessions are presented using 'recipe' style instructions because we believe, from our own experience and that of our consulting teachers, that if you have not used drama before you would probably very much want to be guided through your first encounters with its use. Of course, once you have tried out a few sessions and/or returned to the same session in the next academic year, or with a different class, you might begin to feel more confident and relaxed about using drama in your lessons, and at that point we would encourage you to begin to adapt our instructions to your own particular tastes and needs. Indeed, in the final chapter of this book we provide ideas about ways in which you might like to think about adapting our instructions to give you, the teacher, greater ownership of the material.

Our primary aim is not simply to tell you about how effective drama can be in the teaching of science – although that is certainly part of what we hope to do – but rather to allow you to use drama for yourselves so that you can experience *why* we believe that drama is such an effective means of teaching and learning about science.

Structure

It is probably useful at this point to explain a number of features about the structure of the book. The first point to make is that the sessions were developed, refined and written by different contributing authors, working with different consulting teachers in different types of school, and this individuality comes through clearly in the different styles of writing across, and within, the three subject areas. We see this diversity as a strength in that it allows the reader to gain an appreciation of the fact that, while there are a variety of ways of 'doing drama', there is no single 'right' way. That said, our own experience of working with teachers and trainee teachers is that, as you try out different sessions, by different authors, you might begin to develop a preference for one way of 'doing drama' over another. Yet, while we value this diversity of style and approach, we – and the teachers we consulted – felt that there needed to be some way of ordering the material and ensuring that it would be relatively easy for the reader to move from session to session, even when written by different authors.

Our consulting teachers felt that it would be extremely useful if the sessions were to be grouped, not only by subject, but also in terms of the UK's unique Key Stages. While we agreed that grouping the sessions by subject was ideal, we had some misgivings about the use of Key Stages, given the international nature of the readership and the fact that many readers would have little, if any, knowledge of these. During subsequent discussions with teachers, both in the UK and internationally, it was felt that the best way forward would be to group the sessions for each subject into two separate chapters, one of which would contain sessions relevant to the age range 11–14, and the other for the age range 14–16. That said, we would emphasize that these age ranges are illustrative, rather than definitive, and are based on our own personal teaching experiences as well as the views of those teachers who have worked with us both in the UK and abroad. Ultimately, though, it is you the teacher, on the basis of your professional knowledge and experience, who is best placed to decide the appropriateness of any particular session to any one of your classes. Similarly, while we suggest the number of student roles within some of these sessions, this should be seen principally as a guide, rather than a rigid requirement, and one that you can change in light of your own professional understanding of the needs and demands of your students.

Each session starts with a title followed by its aims and outcomes. In view of probable changes to the National Curriculum in the UK, and the international nature of the intended readership, it was decided not to link these aims to the UK National Curriculum, but to allow the individual teacher to decide how the aims and outcomes that are suggested with each session fit into their own lesson objectives and intended outcomes.

We have suggested a suitable location for the activity as well as providing a list of resources you will need based on our suggested number of students taking part. We list common misconceptions that we, and the teachers we have worked with, have found that students can bring to these sessions as well as misconceptions that the drama could potentially generate.

Most of the sessions in chemistry and biology, and some in physics, suggest one of six generic warm-up activities that can be used to help students get into a frame of mind to use the ensuing drama activities more effectively. Full details of all six warm-up activities, and how to use them, are contained at the back of the book. Within the physics chapters, in particular, there are some sessions in which the authors wanted to use warm-up activities designed to be an integral part of the main activity, rather than using one of the generic warm-up activities.

After detailing the warm-up activity, instructions for the main activity are provided which, in turn, is followed by a section on differentiation and how the activity can be adapted to cater for different attainment levels. Each session ends with a 'points to watch out for' section that deals specifically with associated health and safety issues.

Time wise, these sessions are, generally speaking, *not* designed to take up a whole typical 60-minute lesson, but to fit into a whole lesson on a related topic at a point at which you, the teacher, drawing on your professional judgement, feel it would be most appropriate. For convenience, and to enable the teacher to plan how and when to introduce the session within a planned teaching sequence, each session starts with a guide to the total time required for the complete activity, that is the warm-up *plus* main activity, in addition to which we also provide the time required for the warm-up and main activity separately.

Some sessions are accompanied by photographs, helping teachers see the positioning of students and props. There are additional materials on the continuum website that accompanies this book.

In some cases, sessions have play scripts or additional student worksheets/activities that we have placed on the book's website, to keep materials uncluttered and succinct. These can be adapted by users as they wish to suit their students. You can sign up for access to these online resources at http://education.abrahamsbraund.continuumbooks.com.

Many science teachers will probably be unfamiliar with some of the drama terms and meanings used in this book. Bidi Iredale, one of our two drama experts, who has spent many years working and explaining how drama can be used to teach science to teachers, and trainee teachers alike, has put together some advice and explains some of the terms that are specific to drama.

We firmly believe that no book that sets out to help teachers teach science can hope to do so without explaining to those teachers why the authors believe their book can make a difference and in this respect this book is no different. In the next chapter we look at what research and scholarship have to say about the role of drama in teaching science as well as providing an introduction to a range of drama techniques.

Throughout the book, common hazards and issues to 'watch out for' are suggested. These can be found in boxes within the lesson plans.

When you see this symbol, go to the companion website (http://education.abrahamsbraund. continuumbooks.com) to find downloadable resources to accompany the activities.

The value of using drama to teach science

Ian Abrahams and Bidi Iredale

As science teachers and educators we 'do not only want to know facts and to understand relations for the sake of knowledge, we want to know and understand in order to be able to act and act "better" than we did before' (Langeveld, 1965 p. 4). This chapter provides a broad overview of the research and scholarship in this area so as to provide an understanding of *why* and *how* drama can help us to better our teaching of science.

While scientists, who aim to make sense of the world in an empirical and systematic manner, might see little in common with dramatists – who seek to portray or represent the world around them, in fact both groups are fascinated with phenomena. This fascination motivates both scientists and dramatists alike to provide metaphoric and explanatory responses for the phenomena they see and, as Fels and Meyer (1997) note, 'the question "what if" prods scientist and dramatist towards creative exploration and interpretation of experiential, sensual worlds, real and imagined' (p.75).

Yet 'what if' questions also occur to students who, from an early age, encounter new phenomena on a regular basis so that, by the time they arrive at secondary school, they are already proficient at using their senses to learn about and understand the world around them (McCaslin, 1996). It is important to be aware that in this respect students enter the science laboratory not as empty vessels waiting to be 'filled' with scientific knowledge, but as individual minds already full of ideas about the world that are often referred to as either 'misconceptions', 'pre-conceptions' or 'pre-scientific conceptions' (Driver et al., 2000). From the perspective of what has become known as 'constructivism' one of the primary roles of the teacher is to challenge these misconceptions and, in so doing, bring about their re-construction in order to enable the students to 'see' the world in the same 'scientific way' that the teacher 'sees' it (Ogborn et al., 1996).

The problem has been that as traditional pedagogy, involving book learning, writing and recipe-style practical work, has tended to dominate much of science teaching and learning; there has been little guidance available on practical approaches to realizing this 'constructivist approach'. Recently Tytler (2007) called for a wider view of learning that takes account of research and scholarship in the socio-cultural tradition with a particular emphasis on the way in which teachers can promote learning using teaching methods in which groups of learners negotiate meaning together in shared tasks. One group of methods in this tradition uses various forms of drama (enactment, argumentation, role play, mime and dance) to make ideas, theories and processes, at varying degrees of complexity and abstraction, more comprehensible to learners through a more active involvement in their learning in which students are presented with opportunities to try out their ideas, solve problems and develop further understanding and knowledge (Smilansky, 1968).

This is *not* to claim that the use of drama should, or even could, totally, or even substantially, replace other more traditional approaches in teaching science. Rather the suggestion is that an effective learning environment for school science requires, as most science teachers recognize, a variety of teaching and learning approaches and that, within this broad range of approaches, drama can play a significant part. Indeed, drama already plays a prominent part in the teaching of some of the humanities such as English and history and has been recommended as an effective teaching strategy for science teaching (Kentish, 1995; Duveen and Solomon, 1994; Gardner, 1991). Furthermore Kentish (1995) has suggested that an approach requiring students to become personally engaged in their study is more likely to be seen as meaningful to them than one in which they remain 'passive' observers or 'recipients' of someone else's scientific knowledge. If students are allowed to experience the actual personal involvement that the use of drama provides they are far more likely to become personally interested in the material being taught.

Indeed, the generation of personal interest is important because recent studies in the area of personal interest (Renninger, 1998; Schiefele, 1996; Ainley, 1994) have shown that students who undertake a particular activity in which they already have a personal interest will, relative to students with no prior personal interest, be observed to pay closer attention to, learn more from, and engage for longer with, any new material that they are presented with. The positive relationship between personal interest in, and understanding of, a subject or activity arises as a consequence of the fact that a student, as with any individual, will prefer, if given a choice, to study what already interests them (Bergin, 1999). By increasing their understanding of that subject, or activity, they increase their personal interest in it yet further (Alexander, 1997; Deci, 1992), developing what can usefully be thought of as a system of positive feedback. Research by Webb (1980) has also found that undertaking role play allows students to gain a deeper understanding of the scientific ideas, in addition to which the drama appears to provide an 'anchor'(White, 1979) between the scientific ideas and the material contained within the drama activity which results in demonstrable improvements in students' ability to recollect scientific explanations (Duveen and Solomon, 1994). Why this might be the case is, as Erickson (1988) has suggested, that drama has the capacity to engage students using *all* of their senses, thereby presenting the same material through a multiplicity of different approaches which, it seems reasonable to assume, has the advantage of not only reinforcing the learning, but of catering to all types of learners. Furthermore, both Bailey (1993) and Gardner (1991) have both argued that drama can help some students develop their conceptual understanding of what are sometimes highly abstract scientific ideas by linking them directly to ideas with which they are already familiar from their everyday personal experiences. In this respect Stencel and Barkoff (1993) have suggested that drama can be a particularly powerful tool for bridging the conceptual gap between the world of familiar, everyday experience and the unfamiliar as, for example, when students are taught about scientific processes and structures that occur at the atomic and/or molecular level of which they have no prior personal experience.

Drama also offers additional benefits above and beyond helping to develop conceptual understanding. Kentish (1995), for example, has pointed out that the enhanced sense of ownership of the lesson that drama can provide, can foster a much desired development in problem-solving, communication and decision-making skills. Likewise, Butler (1989) has claimed that the use of drama provides a window of opportunity for highly collaborative learning. Indeed, not only does it provide an opportunity for collaborative learning, possibly offering the advantage of peer teaching (Duveen and Solomon, 1994), but it is sufficiently flexible to enable those students who feel intimidated by the idea of taking on active performing roles to become engaged in preparatory work. Such preparatory work can, for example, include sourcing evidence, preparing props or writing scripts, all of which provide valuable learning experiences.

General introduction to using drama in science teaching

Using drama in the teaching of science opens up a whole tool box of techniques with which to engage students, to illustrate and explain scientific concepts, to actively explore scientific theories and to access students' understanding of the science. Drama techniques such as warm-ups, physical theatre, tableaux and role play give you added opportunities to personalize the science for your students. For example, role playing their own experience of 'Forces' from the moment they get up to when they arrive at school (pushing the duvet off the bed, pulling the bedroom door open, being pulled along when you take the dog for its morning walk, giving your mate a friendly shove, being jostled in the corridor, etc.) enables students to make a direct personal connection between the science and their own experiences. By taking the science off the page, out of the book, down from the white board and onto the classroom or science lab floor and using a student's body, instead of pen and paper, means learning and understanding take place on a physical and kinetic level. Students can become an electron, the stomach, an ion, a leaf or an ammeter.

In my experience drama activities can work just as well in classes where challenging behaviour and attitudes exist as in classes of well behaved, highly motivated students. Similarly, drama activities can improve the engagement in science of the more reticent, quiet students who will avoid being drawn into the lesson by hiding behind their good behaviour and politeness. In drama there are no observers and in many of the exercises everyone has to actively participate. The drama demands that everyone joins in – there is no other option – so more reticent students are not able to get away with 'behaving' and daydreaming their way through the lesson. This is just as important an application of the drama techniques as engaging with unruly, boisterous students.

At the same time you are given a different way to assess students' learning and understanding of a science topic. For example you can, after carrying out scientific investigations into 'dissolving', ask students to present their results in a series of frozen images that they need to explain to the rest of the class.

The science through drama techniques I have successfully used are:

- Focusing games
- Tableaux/Freeze frame
- Animated diagrams
- Role play

Focusing games

There are six focusing, or warm-up, exercises explained in detail in Appendix 1 (see page 125) that you can use in conjunction with the subject-specific role plays in this book. Each exercise or game has been tried and tested and developed in the classroom or science lab, with teachers and their students. As you become more familiar with these there is no reason for you not to experiment and see whether you prefer using a different example to the one we have suggested.

Tableaux/Freeze frame

This is a technique using a still image to show or explore the science being studied, like a photograph or a freeze frame on a dvd. It is a good way to get students to think of examples of when and how they experience the science in their own lives. Once a basic tableau has been made, it can be further developed and added to in order to explore the science further. It really works if you can make it clear that the images the students make are 'still' images, as when the freeze frame button has been pushed on the dvd player, no-one moves.

To introduce the idea of tableaux make use of the following 'Mill, grab and tab' exercise.

1. The group walks around the space. The leader calls out a number and the players have to get into groups of that number.
2. In these groups the players are given an image they have to make – without any discussion between them – in the time it takes the leader to count down from five to one.
3. Initially choose a very simple image, for example 'a dentist and a patient'. Without conferring, the players make this image and are still/frozen by the time you reach one.
4. To share the tableaux at this point you can ask half the room to relax while the other half hold their positions for all to see. Then swap over.
5. After each tableau is completed the players move around the room until you call out another number and another image. Call out a different number each time so the players have to work in groups of different sizes and with different people.
6. Call out an object which must be made in a frozen image or tableau e.g. a mug of tea, a toaster, a hair dryer, a fridge, etc.

Once the players have got to grips with the technique you can ask them in their final groupings to make a tableau of the science being studied. At this point, the players may confer in order to make a more complex tableau.

When studying 'Forces' the players can be asked to make an image of how they experience force in their own lives. In this instance they may make images of pushing open a door, someone pushing someone over, pushing a broken down car, pulling a friend away from a fight, etc. When each group has created a good, clear, tableau it is shown to the rest of the class and is used as a focus of discussion. The tableaux can then be developed further in a variety of ways to explore the subject and to involve more people in one tableau.

Labelling

The rest of the group can add to the tableaux by verbally labelling a tableau or by making written labels and using metre rules to annotate the tableau. These labelled tableaux can be photographed and the photographs stuck into exercise books to act as a diagram and to jog the students' memories.

Adding to the tableaux

More people can be added to the tableau to show the direction of the force (by pointing) and the magnitude of the force (by decreasing or increasing the length of the pointing arm and showing the magnitude in their facial expressions!).

Sounds and words

The groups can be asked to put sound effects to their tableau, or speak one sentence each explaining what they are in the tableau.

Change

The groups can be asked to make changes to their tableaux. For example, to make a tableau showing a balanced or equal force into an unbalanced, or unequal force or to change the direction of the force in the tableau.

Extended tableaux

The tableaux can be extended by asking players to add a 'before' tableau and an 'after' tableau. For example, when studying acid rain groups make 'before', 'during' and 'after' tableaux to show how acid rain effects the atmosphere or the environment.

Animated diagrams

This technique is used to bring a diagram off the page and animate it. It helps to understand the different parts of a diagram. It can also be used to present tables or graphs and information in a different way, to engage in a more physical and visual way of learning and to use physical memory. Human diagrams can be further developed and animated to become role play.

Choose a diagram or table that you want to study and explore further. The aim is to lay out the diagram in the room using people, and be able to move the parts of the diagram to explain and explore it further. Elements of the diagram can begin as tableaux and movements and sounds, etc. can be added. In its simplest form I have used this technique to lay out a human thermometer across a room with students making tableaux of examples of things at different temperatures along the thermometer, or to make a representation of the electromagnetic spectrum.

Role play

This method further develops the animated diagrams and tableaux and, not only aids in presenting and remembering information, but also uses science knowledge and understanding. Role play is really useful where there is a journey of any kind – as in food moving through the digestive system, blood transporting things around the body, heat being transferred, etc. By walking these paths themselves and creating the processes along the way, students engage their physical memory and also have to be very clear in their understanding of the processes they are role playing.

The role play can be teacher-led and executed by the whole class together, with roles being handed out by the teacher and everyone contributing the best way to show what is happening. Smaller groups can also be given the task to work independently to create part of the role play and then the teacher can put the whole piece together at the end of the session. For example, smaller groups could be given the task to represent what happens in different parts of the digestive system, e.g. mouth, gullet, stomach, intestine and so forth. When all the groups have satisfactorily completed these representations they can be put in the correct order, and a volunteer 'piece of food' can be sent down the line to experience what happens to food in the digestive system.

Each part of the role play has to be broken down into its constituent parts. Each part of the journey – and the processes that occur along the way – has to be identified and represented in a clear form. So at the beginning of the digestive system, the mouth has to be broken down into the teeth, the chewing action and the introduction of the enzyme in the saliva, etc.

The addition of sound effects, words, characterization and attitude really brings role play to life. The blood in the blood stream waiting for nutrition could be enticing and beckoning the food in a greedy manner, making hungry noises or calling out, 'come on, come on'. When looking at thermal transfer, good insulators can be surly and turn their backs on heat energy, and shun them, while good conductors can be really friendly and call out eagerly to heat energy. This characterization and attitude add humour and personalize the role play for the students and make it even more memorable.

General tips

- Follow the instructions as they are designed to make the exercises work.
- Do not be afraid to stop, or interrupt, an exercise if the instructions are not being followed, as the end result will be so much clearer and more satisfactory if they are followed.
- If possible try out the exercise among yourselves as a science department first.
- Be creative in changing and adapting the exercises.
- Have fun!

This chapter has discussed some of the research and scholarship which indicate that drama can offer teachers and students alike many benefits, not only in terms of teaching and learning science, but also in developing a wider range of skills and abilities. It has also provided an overview of the structure of the book and an introduction to the techniques that are used.

In the following chapters we provide clear, step-by-step guidance on class-tested examples so that teachers with little, or no, experience of using drama within their science lessons can make use of what is a rich and rewarding method of teaching science.

2 Biology: session plans for 11–14

This chapter contains the following session plans

Adaptation and survival • Martin Braund

Total time 20 minutes

Aims and outcomes

- To learn that prey animals have behavioural adaptations to survive predation.
- To observe patterns resulting from different animal behaviour and make and test predictions.
- To learn about outcomes of animal behaviour.

Location

Ideally in a room where you can create space for circles of 10–12 students by moving tables or in a school hall or outside (on a still day).

Resources required

Bean bags or screwed-up black and white paper balls to represent the blackbirds, secure blindfold and small bell fixed or sewn onto a woolly hat. Note: Some schools have gone to the extent of making headgear with ears and facial features for the sparrowhawk, owl and mouse to wear which gives younger students an additional sense of fun and realism.

Misconceptions

The game might generate ideas of anthropomorphic determinism, e.g. that trees consciously 'decide to make a noise' so as to 'protect the blackbirds'.

Process

Warm-up: Throwing birds (5 minutes)

A circle of children practises throwing the birds to each other. You should start by one student throwing one bird to another student at an opposite part of the circle and then you can introduce another bird and so on, until you have about five to nine birds flying (being thrown) across and around the circle. It is useful for throwers and receivers (the trees) to maintain eye contact and to train all students to maintain alertness.

Activity (15 minutes)

Outline

The activity is provided as two parts. Both or either of the parts of the activity can be used. In these activities a circle of about 10–15 students act as a woodland of trees. In the middle of this wood, within the circle, is a clearing. In part one a student is chosen to act as a predator, the sparrowhawk. The sparrowhawk stands in the middle of the circle (the clearing) and tries to catch one of the blackbirds as they are flying across the clearing from one tree to another (being thrown from one side of the circle to the other).

Birds flying inside the circle of trees and the 'sparrow hawk' trying to catch one.

With one bird being thrown from one side to the other it is quite easy for the sparrowhawk to capture the blackbird but this gets much more difficult to do when there are two, three, four or more birds flying across the circle. This simulates the benefits of flocking behaviour. The game can be changed by getting students to throw the blackbirds shorter distances around the inner edges of the circle, showing that shorter distances of flight around the open spaces help survival (which is how blackbirds often behave. They also fly quite low across open spaces – watch them in your garden if you have one). The introduction by the teacher of a 'white blackbird' as one of several birds flying around the circle helps show the selective disadvantages of albinism as the sparrowhawk often finds it easier to select or catch a white variant.

In part two of the game the sparrowhawk is replaced by a student, who is blindfolded, as an owl. Another student, wearing a hat with a small bell attached, enters the circle after the owl has been blindfolded and acts a mouse. The mouse must creep around within the clearing without being caught by the owl. The game can be repeated by getting the trees to make wind noises, first very softly and then increasing in volume – simulating how much more difficult predation is on windy nights.

Instructions

1. Arrange 10–15 students in a circle. The diameter of the circle should be about 4m or at a size that is comfortable for students to be spaced out but be able to throw and catch the blackbirds. Tell them that they represent trees in a wood and that the inside of the circle space is a clearing in the wood.
2. Get students to practise throwing and receiving the birds (warm-up exercise)
3. Ask one student to be the sparrowhawk, explaining that they must enter the circle and must try to catch the blackbird in flight. They are not allowed to grab or take it from any of the trees (if your sparrowhawk is too good at catching birds tell them they can only use one hand!).
4. As the game proceeds introduce more blackbirds one at a time to different trees. If you have several circles of students you will need one person to act as the teacher/supervisor for each group.
5. Debrief the activity as a class or carry out the second part of the task and then do a debrief of both parts of the activity. Discussion points should draw out: relative predation successes related to blackbird/mouse behaviour and/or environmental conditions.

Note: Students might throw birds too vigorously across the circle so that they fall and the sparrowhawk just picks them up. On the other hand a slow, leisurely lob across the circle often means that an astute and quick sparrowhawk can easily catch the bird – but this can be a discussion point about the patterns of predation seen in the game.

Differentiation

A white albino mutant blackbird can be introduced to the first part of the game to simulate the selective disadvantage of mutants to predation that can occur. It is often easier for the predator to see a lighter bird among a flock. The discussion can draw out that, in this case, the selective disadvantage means mutant albino variants are less likely to survive to pass on their genes to the next generation so albinism in the population of blackbirds remains rare.

> **Watch out for:** Take care with silliness, pushing, etc. while students are moving around.

Microbes – the fight against disease • Martin Braund

Total time 60 minutes

Aims and outcomes

- To learn that natural defences of the body against microbe attack can be enhanced through contact with a similar or attenuated microbe (vaccination).
- To explore how creative application of scientific ideas can bring about technological developments (developments in medicine).
- To examine ethical and moral implications of using and applying science.

Location

In the classroom or laboratory.

Resources required

 Copies of script for the play *The Discovery of Vaccines* and copies of the student activities available to download from: http://www.sycd.co.uk/who_am_i/everywhere/drama.htm

Misconceptions

Students might think vaccination is the injection of the virulent, active form of a microbe. The story of the play should help address this by showing that body contact with an attenuated or weaker microbe (bacteria) of anthrax stimulates the production of antibodies that are active in protecting against the more virulent, fully active version of the microbe.

Process

Warm-up (10 minutes)

Two truths and one lie (see page 131). The focus could be on infections and diseases.

Activity (15 minutes for reading/rehearsal + 10 minutes for class play performance or reading + 15 minutes for second group to read/perform if needed + follow-up student activities: 10 minutes. Total activity time 50 minutes)

Outline

Students read or play act roles described in the script of a play telling the story of how Louis Pasteur discovered a treatment for the bacterial disease anthrax in 1881. The play script was made freely available by the ASE as part of Science Year in 2000. A play, *The Plague at Eyam* is also available for download and can be used in a similar way as a prelude or alternative to this lesson. It is also advisable to have told the story of Jenner's discovery of 'vaccination' against small pox in 1796.

Instructions

1. Give a short introduction to the task, asking if students can remember being vaccinated against any diseases. Tell them that through reading or performing the play they will learn how the effects of vaccination were explained and could then be more widely used to save life.
2. Depending on the number of students in the class, divide them into suitably sized groups to read or perform the whole play or to read/perform different scenes. The script has parts for 16 students arranged as casts for three groups of scenes.
3. Give time for allocation of roles and to read the introduction and the parts or to rehearse the play. Help students with any difficult words.
4. Read/perform the play as a class or allow several repeated performances if there is more than one group.
5. Carry out the suggested student activities and allow time for completion. Alternatively, these could be set for homework.

Note: Students who are shy to read or who have speech disabilities can be included as prompters or non-participant extras if the play is performed. Encourage students to read clearly and slowly so they can easily be heard by the rest of the class.

Questions to help pupils reflect on what they have learned from the simulation are available on page 134 and online.

Differentiation

Differentiation is mainly through help given to different students. Differentiate the allocation of parts depending on the reading abilities of students but encourage reluctant students to participate and praise their efforts. Some questions on the activity sheet are more challenging than others.

Human reproduction – fertilization • Martin Braund

Total time 13 minutes

Aims and outcomes

- To learn that fertilization involves the fusion of the nuclei of sperm and egg.
- To realize that the sex of the foetus is decided by the chromosome (X or Y) present in the sperm nucleus fertilizing the ovum.

Location

Classroom/lab space, drama studio, hall or outside.

Resources required

Two sheets of A1 paper with a big (approx. 1m-diameter) circle drawn onto them. A sheet of A4 paper for each student, each bearing a large letter X or Y.

Misconceptions

Students sometimes think fertilization is only the moment at which the sperm reaches the surface membrane of the ovum rather than completion of mixing of genetic material from the sperm and egg nuclei. This drama should help address this.

Process

Warm-up (5 minutes)

Hand circle (see page 127).

Activity (3 minutes to brief students and 5 minutes to carry it out. Total activity time 8 minutes)

Outline

Students act as sperm carrying X or Y chromosomes and race to fertilize a student acting as the ovum nucleus. A few other students act as the membrane surrounding the egg. This is a relatively short exercise performed as a starter or plenary activity in a lesson on human reproduction and fertilization.

Instructions

1. Give a short introduction to the task stating that this dance/movement exercise is to help understand what happens in human fertilization and how the sex of 'the baby' is determined.
2. One girl student carrying a letter X acts as the ovum nucleus and stands at the centre of a large circle at one side of the lab, hall or playground. A number of students not carrying letters loosely link hands and stand around the circumference of the circle, representing the ovum membrane.
3. The rest of the class are told to stand in a line some distance away. Boys each carry a letter Y and girls each carry a letter X. It is best to have equal numbers of each. Each child represents one spermatazoon cell.
4. The teacher says 'go' and all spermatozoa move by 'fairy steps', heel to toe, heel to toe, as quickly as possible to get to the ovum. Any students who cheat, run or fall over are pronounced 'dead' and have to sit out of the race.
5. The first sperm to reach the outer wall of the ovum can enter the ovum through the circle of students acting as a membrane by crawling through a gap between them. The circle of students must let this sperm through but then close up so that no more sperm can get through. The successful student (sperm) gives his or her letter to the student representing the ovum nucleus.
6. The students playing the ovum membrane sit down and the student playing the fertilized zygote holds up the letters so the rest of the class can see and the class have to shout 'boy' or 'girl'.
7. The exercise can be repeated a few times to see what happens after other turns.

8. The class are asked questions about when fertilization occurs and harder (differentiated) questions about what happens when more than one sperm hits the ovum membrane surface, what slows up sperm in the real situation and where exactly the ovum might be fertilized in the reproductive tract (fallopian tube or womb).

Note: Beware that some students might try to break the rules of taking 'fairy steps'. Most students, except those with severe physical disabilities, should be able to take part as sperm and no running is involved but anyone should be able to play ovum nucleus.

The ovum has been fertilized and no more spermatozoa can enter.

Differentiation
Questions to the class can be selected or designed to take account of the content covered before the exercise or of students' perceived abilities.

> **Watch out for:** Take care with silliness, pushing, etc. while students are moving around.

Muscles and movement – features (adaptations) of animals without backbones • Martin Braund

Total time 16 minutes

Aims and outcomes

- To learn that animals without backbones and legs, like worms, often move by alternate rhythmic contractions of groups of their muscles.

Location

Classroom/lab space, drama studio, hall or outside.

Resources required

None

Misconceptions

Students often think animal muscles can only work like the paired (antagonistic) muscles in humans. In many invertebrates muscles are arranged as blocks or in circles, as in the earthworm.

Process

Warm-up (5 minutes)

Hand circle (see page 127).

Activity (2 minutes to brief students and practise and 5 minutes to carry out the activity and a further 4 minutes for the extension movement activity if used. Total activity time 11 minutes)

Outline

Students form a human chain to simulate the action of the worm's muscles as they move forwards. The exercise is best done with 15 or more students.

The movement of an earthworm.

Instructions

1. Clear a space so that a line of 15 or more students has space to move forwards.
2. Ask each student to grasp the waist of the person in front of them (use the warm-up activity to help students get used to this idea).
3. The students are told that the first three to five people must squeeze in and the next three to five students must stretch out and so on, until the end of the worm.
4. Tell the students that they must do this slowly and not to over-stretch or over-squeeze.
5. The students should repeat the exercise but this time each set of three to five reverses what they did last time – the squeezers stretch and the stretchers squeeze!
6. Try this and, if the students do it correctly, the worm (line of students) should move forwards!
7. Keep repeating with the teacher calling the changes – the worm should continue to move forwards.

Note: Watch out for students trying to do these tasks too quickly or without practising in sets what they must do before forming up the worm.

Differentiation

This simulation shows longitudinal extension of the worm by muscle action. If you want to show circular contractions and extensions get the students to work in pairs facing each other with their arms held but as straight as possible. One group of three to five students then stretches their arms out laterally in the direction of the line and the next set stretches their arms out at right angles to the line and so on – the worm should move forwards.

Follow-up or preparatory activities

The simulation could form part of a lesson in which students have first observed worms moving either first hand or on a video or film, for example: http://www.youtube.com/watch?v=37Jl2TcdbiQ. As a follow-up activity real specimens of earthworms can be placed onto a sheet of plain paper and the class told to be silent. Using a paper cone 'ear trumpet' or by getting close to the worm they should hear a rustling sound. This is tiny pairs of 'setae' or hairs on the underside of segments that help the worm grip against soil. On the paper they are slipping – hence the rustling sound. Looking at the underside of an earthworm with a binocular microscope or electronic micro camera to see the setae and muscle movements more clearly is also very rewarding.

> **Watch out for:** Take care with silliness, pushing, etc. while students are moving around.

Human digestive system • Martin Braund

Total time 35 minutes

Aims and outcomes

- Learn the functions of different regions and organs of the human gut.

Location

In cleared space in a classroom or laboratory.

Resources required

Cards, balloons, boxes or molecular models for the final activity.

Misconceptions

The role play might give an oversimplified notion of digestion. The relative sizes and relations of organs to each other will need discussion by the teacher.

Process

Warm-up (5 minutes)

Hand circle (see page 127).

Activity (30 minutes)

Outline

Groups of three to four students are given one part of the gut system to play: mouth, oesophagus, stomach, small intestine, large intestine, rectum, anus. They revise or obtain information on what their part does and how it does this. After rehearsal, each group performs and the teacher and whole class uses 'freeze frame' to critique each group's enactments and provide feedback so that groups refine their efforts. Groups then come together as one whole gut system and food (in the shape of models, balloons, boxes, cards) is passed along the gut so that the whole process from ingestion of food to excretion of waste is modelled and seen.

A group of students stimulates peristalsis along the oesophagus (gullet).

Instructions

1. Divide the class into groups of three to four students and allocate each group an organ: mouth, oesophagus, stomach, small intestine, large intestine, rectum, anus.

2. Allow each group about 5 minutes to rehearse how they will portray the actions and functions of their organ.

3. Ask each organ group to perform without telling the rest of the group which organ they are portraying. The class has to say what organ they are seeing and why they think it is a good representation of that organ.

4. The teacher can ask a group to replay their organ and can use 'freeze frame' to stop the action, asking the group to explain what an action or movement shows.

5. After all groups have performed, they are asked to assemble as a whole gut, under the direction of the teacher, in order from mouth to anus.

6. Food items (boxes, balloons and so on) are passed into the mouth and the gut has to process the food all along the gut until it is excreted from the anus. As soon as one food item leaves the oesophagus, then another item can be introduced to the mouth to keep the action going.

Note: It is important to keep the whole of the gut model 'parts' (groups) busy and this can de done by continually passing different types of food items into the mouth. Some students with special learning needs can be used as observers or 'feeders'.

Differentiation

To add to the complexity of the simulated gut model you can ask groups to perform functions of the liver, the circulatory system (blood capillaries next to the gut walls), the pancreas and gall bladder.

For older students or more advanced classes you could add absorption of food chemicals to the model. Absorbed molecules such as glucose, water, fatty acids and amino acids, shown using cards, different coloured balloons or molecular models for the different food chemicals, could be shown alongside those that are too large to be absorbed such as lipids, larger proteinaceous molecules, starch and so on. Alternatively, groups could devise their own ways of showing the roles of digestive enzymes, bile and the gut wall in the processes of digestion for a particular organ.

> **Watch out for:** Students can sometimes get overly excited by this activity so it is advisable to remind them to take care.

Circulatory and respiratory systems • Sandra Campbell

Total time 35 minutes

Aims and outcomes

- To learn that life processes are supported by the organization of cells into tissues, organs and body systems.

Location

Can be carried out in a clear space in the lab. The school hall or playground would provide more space.

Resources required

Cards labelled for each character. For the basic role play you will need The Heart, The Lungs, The Blood, and The Legs. These can be written on large stickers, but A5 cards worn on strings around the neck are more visible and can be re-used.

If you plan a more advanced role play you may need cards for The Gut, The Brain, The Arms and The Liver and tokens, made from A5 card, clearly labelled Carbon Dioxide, Oxygen and Waste Products. For a basic role play a minimum of three of each will be needed. For a more advanced role play tokens labelled Water and Glucose can be used too.

Misconceptions

Careful consideration needs to be given not to reinforce the misconceptions that diffusion is an active process as the tokens are passed over and that the Energy Released cards (see Differentiation) do not portray energy as a substance such as carbon dioxide and water (cards can be colour-coded to these substances).

Process

Warm-up (5 minutes)

Fruit salad (see page 126). Names of parts of the circulatory system could be used.

Activity (30 minutes)

Outline

The lead-in to the role play could involve students making their labels, cards or stickers for the action – additional time is needed for this. In the basic role play the students are given a key phrase to act out. If used as a revision activity, this can be less prescriptive with the students given the labels and the tokens and encouraged to devise their own scenarios.

 Instructions

Storyline, suggested script and actions

Character 1:
The Heart   I am the heart. I am the pump that pushes blood around the body.

Heart beat can be simulated by the Heart, standing and flexing knees to bob up and down, gently pushes Character 2: the Blood, towards Character 3: the Lungs.

Character 3:
The Lungs   I am the lungs.
The Blood   At the lungs I pick up oxygen and pass over carbon dioxide. I then return to the heart.

The Blood student walks to Character 3: the Lungs, where they exchange tokens for Carbon Dioxide and Oxygen. The Blood walks back to the Heart, carrying an Oxygen token.

Character 1:
The Heart   I push the blood carrying oxygen to other parts of the body, such as the legs.

The Blood student walks to Character 4: the Legs.

Character 4:

The Legs   I am the legs. My muscles are respiring. I need to take oxygen from the blood and give carbon dioxide to the blood. I also need glucose from the blood so that I can respire. I pass waste products to the blood.

The Legs student jogs gently on the spot and gives tokens for Carbon Dioxide and Waste Products to the Blood, and receives Oxygen and Glucose tokens from the Blood. The Blood returns to the Heart and is pushed to the Lungs, repeating the cycle, with more exchange of tokens.

Carbon dioxide is exchanged from the Legs to the Blood.

Note: Experience suggests that the students need to be reminded to show their tokens to their audience as they exchange them or what they are exchanging may not be clear to the audience.

Sometimes a more complex role play is not clear to the audience. Encourage students to make their token exchange clear. This part can be re-run as a mime.

Differentiation

This is the role play in its basic form. It is easy to adapt with more cards and more tokens to add, such as:

- Other organs – the gut, brain and liver. This is particularly useful as a revision activity that links together the circulatory, the respiratory and the digestive systems.
- Other processes – separate students can be given Diffusion, Respiration and Energy Released tokens.

Giving some blank labels and the opportunity to discuss and plan the role play makes it less prescriptive. Two students can act together to represent the two sides of the heart, which reinforces the concept of a double circulation. Some students may pick up on the idea that the heart itself needs to respire.

> **Watch out for:** The Heart's pushing should be gentle or mimed. If the labels are to be worn around the neck, weak 'lanyards' of wool or string knotted through card should be used.

Insect pollination • Sandra Campbell

Total time 35 minutes

Aims and outcomes

- To learn the processes and stages involved in the pollination of flowers by insects.

Location

Best performed outside or in a hall. Can be carried out in a clear space in the laboratory.

Resources required

The equipment below is sufficient to represent one bee and two flowers each with five sepals, five petals, three stamens and one carpel:

- Five headbands made from green card (sepal-shaped) to show the five sepals.
- Five headbands made from brightly coloured card (petal-shaped) OR coloured sports bibs to represent the petals.
- Three stamens: filament and anther OR students holding balloons to represent stamens.
- One carpel: ovary style and stigma labels. A woolly hat to represent a mature stigma.
- One bee label or striped tabard or costume of striped material with wings and antennae. If the bee costume has some Velcro attached this can be used to carry the pollen grains.
- Paper balls (available from craft suppliers) OR circles made from pipe cleaners which have small strips of Velcro attached to represent the pollen grains.
- Bin liners or mats for students to kneel on (optional).

Misconceptions

Bees visit flowers not only to collect pollen to eat and feed to their larvae, but to collect nectar. Some nectar is made into honey. (This could be added to the role play.) Some students may be left with the impression that it is the intention of the bee to pollinate the flower. Students often confuse pollination and fertilization and this role play provides the opportunity to address this misconception.

Process

Warm-up (5 minutes)

Fruit salad (see page 126). Names of parts of the plant could be used.

Activity (30 minutes)

Outline

In this role play the students take on the roles of the parts of the flower and a pollinating insect – a bee. If two flowers are used cross-pollination can be shown. The two flowers can be arranged a few metres apart. The role play starts with the flower as a bud. One carpel and three stamens crouch down together surrounded by a ring of five kneeling petals. Facing inwards, five sepals stand in a ring around the other parts of the flower with their arms extended inwards to form a protective roof. As the bud begins to open the sepals walk slowly backwards a few paces and sit down behind the petals. At the same time the petals and sepals shuffle backwards as the flower opens and the carpel and stamens 'grow' to a kneeling position. There should be some space available for the bee to visit the inner parts of the flower.

The narration can be put onto laminated cards for the students to read out. Alternatively, students can be given the narration of the story or a diagram and description of the process of pollination and they work out how to show the action themselves.

Instructions

Suggested script and stage directions

1.

Sepals   We are the sepals. We support and protect the flower when it is in bud. It's a summer's day and this flower is about to open.

The sepals walk slowly backwards a few paces and sit down behind the petals. At the same time the petals and sepals shuffle backwards as the flower opens and the carpel and stamens 'grow' to a kneeling position.

2.

Petals   We are the petals. We attract the bee to the flower. It's several days later and the flower is now fully open.

Bee comes to buzz around the flower.

Insect pollination.

3.

Stamens   We are the stamens. Our top part is the anther where the pollen is made. Today we are mature and holding lots of pollen.

The anthers hold some pollen grains up near their heads.

4.

Carpel   I am the carpel. Here is the stigma where the pollen grains can land. When I am mature I have a sticky stigma.

Puts on the woolly hat to represent a sticky stigma.

5.

Bee   I am the bee. I am an insect that pollinates. What very attractive petals! I travel from flower to flower to collect pollen. I like to eat pollen and feed it to the larvae back in the beehive. Some of pollen gets stuck to me.
   Another colourful flower! I'm going to fly across there to collect some more pollen. Some of the pollen I collected from the first flower rubs off onto the sticky stigma of the second flower. That's pollination. Because it's pollen from one flower going across and landing on the stigma of a different flower it's called cross-pollination.

Stamens add pollen grains to the bee. These can be stuck onto Velcro on the bee.

Bee travels to the second flower and transfers pollen to the woolly hat of the sticky stigma of the second flower.

Insect pollination of a flower (the boy wearing the woollen hat acts as the stigma).

Differentiation

A key-word glossary and pictures and diagrams of the structure of the main parts of an insect pollinated flower can be studied prior to the role play. Students could be asked to write their own script or role cards for the functions of the different structures. The role play can be extended to include fertilization, in which case the 'sticky stigma' could catch a pollen grain in a disposable cup or yoghurt pot to which a pollen tube, made from one leg of a pair of nylon tights, has been affixed. The pollen tube can 'grow' down (unroll) to a container representing the ovary, to represent fertilization.

The idea of stigma maturity can be discussed. If the stigma is not ripe at the same time as the anthers of the same flower then this reduces the opportunity for self-fertilization.

Ask the students how this role play could be modified to model wind pollination.

> **Watch out for:** Take care with silliness and pushing while students are moving around.

Biology:
session plans for 14–16

This chapter contains the following session plans

Food chains – energy transfer • Martin Braund

Total time 20 minutes

Aims and outcomes

- To learn that energy is dissipated (gets less) at each level of a food chain or web and so less is available in food for consumers.
- To make measurements of 'energy' available at the start and end of a food chain.
- To make and test predictions about energy flow/availability.

Location

Outside – playground or field.

Resources required

Four plastic drinks cups each with a 6mm hole drilled at the centre of the base. Two plastic buckets – one containing a measured amount of water, e.g. 5 litres. A large plastic measuring jug or measuring cylinder.

Misconceptions

Students often think energy is destroyed at each nutritional level of an ecosystem rather than being dissipated, e.g. as heat loss or used by living things for their life processes via respiration. If the game is played on the playground it is more obvious that water (energy) has been spilled and so still 'exists' (i.e. has not been destroyed).

Process

Warm-up (5 minutes)

Psst! (see page 129). Statements about 'who eats who' could be used.

Activity (15 minutes)

Outline

Students play a game in which water is transferred from a full bucket along a 'fire bucket chain' of plastic cups to an empty bucket. The amount of water in the bucket at the start represents energy in the sun and the amount of water transferred into the bucket at the end represents energy available at the final level of a food chain, i.e. to the top consumer. Each plastic cup has a hole in the bottom through which water escapes representing that energy is lost (dissipated or used) at each level of transfer or trophic level along the food chain. The final energy at the end of the bucket chain is only a small amount compared with the energy at the start.

Passing 'energy' along the food chain.

Instructions

1. Arrange students in teams of six in a line over about 25m. One student is in charge of the empty bucket and one of the full bucket and the other four students are spaced at regular intervals of 5m.

2. The game starts as the first student takes water in her/his cup and transfers it to the second student who must stand still in their place until the water has been transferred into their cup. The second student does the same to student 3 and so on until student 4 transfers the water (if there is any left!) to the empty bucket at the other end of the chain.

3. Get students to guess how much water (of the original amount) has been transferred to the originally empty bucket. The team transferring the most water is the winner.

4. Repeat the game for three goes or as desired (if the students are not too wet!).

5. Back in the classroom, debrief the activity as class discussion and then carry out the student activity.

Questions to help pupils reflect on what they have learned from the simulation are available on page 135 and online.

Differentiation

Different teams can be given cups with different sized holes or capacities and the results compared. The percentages of water lost can be calculated and graphed for each team and compared to different types of ecosystem and energy dissipation rates.

Watch out for: If students run too fast or hold the cups too near to them they will spill water over themselves. It is best to run with the cup held at arm's length. Any students with known heart or respiratory problems should supervise the buckets or act as recorders. With a 'lively' class you may wish to have one team at a time carrying out the activity while the other students observe and record what happens.

Kidney transplants – homeostasis • Martin Braund

Total time 60 minutes

Aims and outcomes

- To learn that chemical signals enable body systems (urinogenital) to respond to internal and external changes in order to maintain optimal state (maintain water balance).
- To know that contemporary scientific and technological developments have benefits, drawbacks and risks.
- To appreciate the role of the scientific community in ethical and social issues and how people make decisions based on scientific advice but also balance these with personal issues and beliefs.

Location

Lab or classroom.

Resources required

All materials and briefing cards to support and follow up the role play can be downloaded from the 'geneticfutures' website at: http://www.geneticfutures.com/pig/story5.asp. Alternatively, students can work online in the lesson if computers are available.

Misconception

Likely misconceptions are about transplant technology called *xenotransplantation* – transplanting of an organ from another animal species into a human. Assumptions are often made that a transplanted organ might confer other characteristics of the animal to the recipient, hence cartoons criticizing the technology feature patients with pig's ears and snouts. The history of science is replete with similar images, for example Jenner and his patients were depicted as cows after his successful development of a vaccine (from cowpox in cows) to treat the human disease smallpox. A discussion of such examples of science, ridiculed or criticized in the media, is a useful way to enhance teaching of 'how science works'.

Process

Warm-up (10 minutes)

Two truths and one lie (see page 131).

Activity (15 minutes reading and preparation (or before the lesson) + 20 minutes for role play + 15 minutes for class discussion/debate: Total activity time 50 minutes)

Outline

This is a two-stage activity based on resources developed by Y Touring Theatre Company funded by the Wellcome Trust's public engagement with science scheme. Y Touring have produced a play called *Pig in the Middle* which tells the story of teenager Ryan Wheeler, a patient on dialysis, and the dilemmas he faces in deciding whether or not to be one of the first patients to receive a transplanted pig's kidney. A group of four students is allocated roles of people involved in Ryan's story (Ryan, his mother, friend Gemma and the doctor treating him). The gender and names of the roles can be changed to suit the gender of participants.

Instructions

1. Students are set as groups of four around a table and allocated roles, randomly or by teacher or student choice.
2. Students prepare for the role play by reading the appropriate character profile from the 'geneticfutures' webpage: http://www.geneticfutures.com/pig/story5.asp and the article '16-year-old school girl leads mass protest against medical trials'.
3. Students can also read 'related stories' (newspaper articles) that are relevant to the role they are playing from the webpage.

4. The students engage in discussion in role as to whether or not Ryan should take up Dr Mayhew's offer of a pig's kidney transplant.

5. After the role play the teacher can draw out through class or group discussion and debate the key ethical, medical and scientific issues emerging from the role plays.

Note: There is a danger that students in role plays leave the frame of the character they are playing and go into a 'personal frame' to represent their own ideas and beliefs rather than those of the character they are supposed to empathize with. With older, mature students this can be discussed before the role play is prepared. The discussion after the role play is very important as it creates the more personal space for a dialogue that encompasses students' own beliefs and values. Instead of class discussion, teachers may wish to allow groups to 'come out of role' after 10 minutes or so to enter into a more personal discussion about the issues that their role play raised. Ideas and differences between groups can still be collated as a class, but for a shorter time or perhaps via a 'blogspot' where students continue their debate. You will find it hard to stop them discussing issues like this.

Differentiation

All students can engage in this role play. Differentiation comes in the amount and depth of the scientific knowledge and understanding about kidney function in osmoregulation and transplantation technology that they are exposed to and can understand. There are plenty of background articles from specialists in biosciences, medicine and surgery and ethics on the webpage as well as links to other web-based resources.

Follow-up or preparatory activities

- The students will get more out of this role play if they have already studied the role of the kidney in osmoregulation and understand how artificial dialysis attempts to replicate the kidney's function but also what the problems caused by dialysis are for patients.

- Preparation reading from the website and other sources can be done before the lesson so that students are ready to engage in the role play from the start of the lesson.

- A full video version of Y Touring's production of the *Pig in the Middle* is available for students to view after their lesson. They can watch this to compare how their discussions and arguments compared with those of the characters in the film.

- There are other contexts and plays available on the 'geneticfutures' website that could be handled in similar ways in biology or citizenship lessons.

Evolution • Martin Braund

Total time 50 minutes

Aims and outcomes

- To learn that variation within species can lead to evolutionary changes.
- To know an example of how uncertainties in scientific knowledge and ideas change over time and about the role of the scientific community in validating these changes.

Location

Lab or classroom.

Resources required

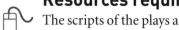

The scripts of the plays and list of follow-up questions for students can be downloaded and printed from the companion website.

Misconceptions

Research has shown that students often subscribe to pre-Darwinian or teleological/deterministic views when it comes to evolution. Thus some students repeat Lamarck's hypothesis that the giraffe got his long neck because *it was necessary* to reach taller trees to get food or believe that animals *purposely* change as the environment does (teleological reasoning). Reading/performing/studying these plays should be followed by discussions that move towards Darwin's view as the most plausible explanation for speciation and evolution. Some debate about recent attempts to use 'intelligent design' to counter Darwin's theory and that many people with religious beliefs hold different world views (sometimes simultaneously with scientific ones) on the origin of species are worth pursuing – see an article on this by Michael Reiss: http://www.newstatesman.com/education/2010/04/science-evolution-creationism.

Process

Warm-up (10 minutes)

Two truths and one lie (see page 131).

Activity (40 minutes)

Outline

This quartet of short plays reflects the development of scientific ideas about evolution in the late nineteenth century and that ideas continue to be the source of argument. Each play can be rehearsed, performed and read by different groups of students or in a sequence by the class, using different students for each play. Background teachers' notes and the scripts for each play can be downloaded from the companion website.

Instructions

1. Students are set as groups depending on the number of roles required for each play.
2. Students read through the script of the play they have been allocated and prepare for reading or performance. Help can be given with any difficult words/concept terms and names.
3. Students read or perform the plays to the rest of the class.
4. Students are given questions about each or all of the plays (this can be set as follow-up or homework). These can be found on the companion website.

Note: Since the plays reflect development of scientific ideas during the nineteenth century, the figures in the original story are predominantly male. In the first and last plays every effort has been made to introduce characters that are female and who have active parts in terms of scientific ideas. In the second and third plays this has not been possible since the characters are of necessity those from history. Teachers should ensure that girls in the groups performing/reading these plays are *not* disadvantaged. They could for example read male leading parts and/or act as narrator or presenter.

Differentiation

All students can take part in these plays. Teachers may want to choose who plays or reads which part depending on their reading abilities. If there are particularly shy students or any with speech disabilities they can take part by playing non-speaking extras to the action or by listening to others and taking notes.

Follow-up or preparatory activities

The plays can be used to teach about evolution at the start of a topic or as revision at the end. The plays could be performed in conjunction with the English or Drama department. They could link with project work in history where students could access information from library and internet sources.

Students could be given plays to read before teaching and could get together in groups to perform them – probably using scripts – but with more rehearsed movements and intonation where appropriate.

Protein synthesis • Sandra Campbell

Total time 30 minutes

Aims and outcomes

- To learn the role of RNA and DNA in protein synthesis.

Location

It is best to use a large space such as a playground that can be marked out with chalk or a school hall or playing field marked out with rope. The activity could be carried out in a clear space in a lab.

Resources required

Cards marked A, T, C, G and U to represent DNA and RNA bases. These can be affixed to clothing with safety pins or worn on headbands. Cards should be made of matching DNA and RNA base pairs (see below).

Lengths of rope or string to represent the backbone of the DNA molecule (suggest this by laying two wavy overlapping strands). Rope or string is also used to show the nuclear membrane, cell membrane and ribosome. Alternatively a student can represent the ribosome.

Chalk (as alternative to rope or string) can be used to draw an outline of the cell and membranes and the ribosome.

Misconceptions

This activity may reinforce the misconception that a small number of amino acids join together to make a protein; it takes at least 50 amino acids to make a protein and many proteins are composed of many thousands of amino acids, so the model falls short in this respect.

Process

Warm-up (5 minutes)

Fruit salad (see page 126). Use names of processes and molecules involved in DNA and RNA replication and cell biology.

Activity (25 minutes)

Outline

The purpose of the activity is to reinforce the concept of protein synthesis through the action of DNA and RNA. The narration and stage directions are provided to give the teacher an idea of how the simulation works. The teacher could revise the sequence with students or provide text and diagrams and, knowing what the props represent, let groups of students devise ways of showing what happens.

 Instructions

Suggested script and stage directions

Narrator When Watson and Crick cracked the structure of DNA they had a problem – they knew that DNA was responsible for making many different types of proteins, but how? They knew it had to be the bases found in DNA that held the code to make proteins. Let's call our bases found in DNA A, T, C and G. Here is a DNA molecule – this part is unzipped and we can see a line of bases.

Stage directions: Six or nine students line up along one 'unzipped' section of the rope representing DNA.

Unzipped DNA bases.

Narrator This is part of the genetic code for making a new protein but the gene can't leave the nucleus. How can we get the information to the ribosome where the protein will be made?

Ribosome situated in the cell cytoplasm.

Narrator We need messenger RNA to help us! This smaller molecule can fit through the pores on the nuclear membrane and transfer the genetic code to the ribosome. Let's see how mRNA is made.

Look at the code. The T of the DNA matches up with an A of messenger RNA, C matches with G, G matches with C. And where we have an A this now matches with U. U is special, it's not in DNA, it's in RNA.

Stage directions: Six, or nine, other mRNA students line up face to face with those representing DNA.

DNA base	Pairs with mRNA base
A	U
T	A
C	G
G	C

The mRNA students hold a length of rope of string to become the RNA molecule.

The bases of messenger RNA align with their corresponding base pairs in DNA.

Narrator   The RNA moves out of the nucleus to one of the ribosomes in the cytoplasm. mRNA moves out (preferably through a pore in the nuclear membrane) to the ribosome.
    Here the ribosome reads the genetic code and joins amino acids together in the correct order. It takes three bases to code for one amino acid.

Stage directions: The first three bases of the RNA are 'read' and an amino acid represented by a student wearing a shaped headband with amino acid on it 'forms'. As the next three bases are read the another amino acid forms, linking hands with the first until a chain of amino acids, 'a protein', is formed. The original mRNA students can return to the nucleus to pick up more genetic code from the DNA.

Narrator   When it is finished the ribosome releases the protein.

Stage directions: Students step away from the ribosome.

Narrator   The protein can leave the cell.

Stage directions: The students representing the protein leave the cell.

Protein synthesis: valine and arginine form the start of a polypeptide chain.

Note: Some students may not wish to hold hands to form the amino acid chain so a string or rope can be used.

Differentiation

More students can be made triplet codes, emphasizing how with four bases a single base code could lead to four different amino acids; a two-base code could lead to 16 different amino acids and a three-base (triplet) code could lead to 64 different amino acids. Able students can be given the names and triplet codes for some real amino acids such as:

Triplet code	Amino acid that this triplet code codes for
C-A-A	valine
G-A-A	leucine
G-C-C	arginine
A-T-G	tyrosine
C-C-C	glycine

Students can then organize for themselves how to make a chain of, say, four amino acids.

Variation: the mRNA students can write their own cards based on the order of the bases in the DNA. If any of the mRNA students choose T this can serve as reminder that the base U is found in mRNA.

> **Watch out for:** Take care with silliness and pushing while students are moving around.

Germ theory • Sandra Campbell

Total time 20 minutes

Aims and outcomes

- To appreciate how early discoveries led to a 'germ theory'.

Location

Can be carried out in a lab or classroom.

Resources required

Papers for Semmelweiss to read. A bowl of water for hand washing and a cloth. Fake blood (optional) and a piece of cloth to represent Peter's shirt tail.

Misconceptions

Semmelweiss was working decades before Pasteur, Lister and others developed the germ theory of disease, so the link can be made between this and his 'cadaverous particles'.

Process

Warm-up

None required

Activity (20 minutes)

Outline

Groups read, rehearse and perform a play about Semelweiss's discoveries.

 Dr Ignaz Semmelweis – The Saviour of Mothers

Characters

Narrator

Ignaz Semmelweis: a doctor working in the maternity clinic at the Vienna General Hospital

Peter: a medical student at the hospital studying obstetrics with Dr Semmelweis

Maria: a midwife at the same hospital

Carla: Maria's friend

Scene 1

Narrator It's May 1847. In a room next to a maternity clinic at the Vienna General Hospital Dr Semmelweis is reading some papers. Peter, a medical student at the hospital, rushes in. His hands have blood on them and he wipes them on the tail of his shirt.

Peter (hurrying and out of breath, wiping his hands on his shirt) Sorry I'm late Dr Semmelweis, it was a particularly busy morning – we had three dead bodies to examine and dissect.

Semmelweis Well, you missed the important announcement. All the medical students who work with me delivering babies are going to wash their hands in chlorinated lime solution before they go to the maternity clinic.

Peter Wash our hands? Before going to the clinic? Why?

Semmelweis Because I've been studying the two clinics at the hospital. The First Clinic, the one that is staffed by the medical students, has three times more deaths than the Second Clinic which is run by the midwives. I've been through everything, just everything . . . . I think that the only major difference is in the people who work there. You medical students come straight from dissecting corpses; you smell of putrid disease, and the midwives don't. So washing your hands in the chlorinated solution may help to get rid of the smell and the poison of the cadaverous particles you are carrying. Use this. (hands Peter a bowl)

Peter	(Dipping his hands into the bowl and wrinkling his nose in disgust. Goes to dry his hands on his shirt tail again. Semmelweis hands him a cloth) I heard a rumour that some women in Vienna would prefer to have their babies on the street rather than attend the First Clinic.
Semmelweis	It's not just a rumour! They know that almost one in eight of the women attending the First Clinic dies of childbed fever –
Peter	(interrupts) – childbed fever! One of the corpses we dissected today had died from childbed fever!
Semmelweis	(jumping up from his chair and washing his own hands in the bowl) It's time we went through to the clinic. Let's go. (they exit together)

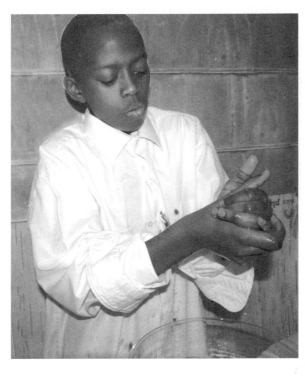

Peter washing his hands in 'chlorinated lime' solution.

Scene 2

Narrator	It's one year later, in 1848. The infection rate at the hospital has dropped dramatically. Two friends, Maria, a midwife at the hospital, and Carla are sitting together in a room in a house in Vienna.
Carla	What's the matter, Maria, you just don't seem happy at the moment?
Maria	(sighs)It's hard to explain, Carla, but I'm worried about my work at the clinic. Do you remember I told you last year about Dr Semmelweis?
Carla	You don't need to remind me! He was the one with all the fancy ideas about handwashing in the maternity clinic. Are you working long hours again and not spending much time with your family?
Maria	The long hours I am used to, it's not that . . .
Carla	Well, has the hospital had begun to accept his ideas about the importance of handwashing with chlorinated lime solution? My cousin died from childbed fever. She had a terrible fever and was in agony for five days. I'd like to think your Dr Semmelweis would find something to stop it – however strange he and his ideas might seem.

Maria	Well, it's true that there are fewer deaths of mothers from childbed fever since we all started washing our hands. Now Dr Semmelweis thinks that washing the medical instruments is important, too. But most people don't believe him. I even overheard one of the doctors shouting and saying that people are put on the Earth to suffer! And that childbed fever helped to remind women of their sins! Another doctor said he was insulted to have to wash his hands – it couldn't possibly be his fault that the mothers were dying.
Carla	Sounds like that doctor's being arrogant! What about the rest of the midwives? Does he have their support?
Maria	Some seem to think it's a good idea. But others are complaining about sore skin from the chlorinated lime solution and all the water they have to carry to make up bowls for handwashing. Now we have to do the instruments too there will be more criticism behind his back.
Carla	What do you think, Maria?
Maria	Last year Dr Semmelweis's good friend Dr Kolletschka died after being wounded by a student's scalpel when they were dissecting a corpse. When they carried out a post-mortem examination of Kolletschka's body it seemed to be diseased in a similar way to the women who had childbed fever.
Carla	(puzzled) But men don't get childbed fever!
Maria	Exactly! This made Dr Semmelweis all the more sure that there is a connection between corpses and childbed fever. He's always muttering about 'cadaverous particles' – something that moves from the corpses to the mothers. He's very angry that he doesn't think the hospital is supporting him enough. I'm proud of him, Carla. I like someone who stands up for their ideas but I'm also worried about the strain that all of this has put him under. What shall I do?
Carla	(thoughtfully) It's hard to know, Maria. It's hard to change people's opinions. Even though there have been many fewer infections in the maternity clinic this year I've heard people say 'it's because of the weather'. Sounds like there's still work to be done.
Maria	(shaking her head sadly) I do worry, Carla. I just hope Dr Semmelweis's big ideas are right.

Note: If fake blood is used it can stain, so a 'shirt tail' of a scrap of cloth should be used.

Differentiation

The medical term for childbed fever (puerperal fever) can be used.

Photosynthesis and the carbon cycle • Sandra Campbell

Total time 25 minutes

Aims and outcomes

- To learn how carbon is assimilated and cycled in the environment.

Location

Can be carried out in a clear space in the laboratory with props on the benches. It can also be carried out in a classroom or hall, without the use of the Bunsen burner 'kiln'.

Resources required

Props	What the prop represents
One large piece of limestone	Limestone cliff
One smaller piece of limestone	Mined rock
Lit Bunsen burner on heatproof mat and tongs	Lime kiln
Molecular models such as Molymod ™ of carbon and dioxide, nitrogen and oxygen	Carbon dioxide, nitrogen, oxygen and glucose
Picture of bird, toy bird, or bird skeleton	A bird
Trough of blue water (use food colouring)	The oceans
Large leaf shape cut out of green sugar paper with a hole cut in the paper that is large enough for the molecular model of carbon dioxide to pass through	A leaf
Trough of green water (use food colouring)	Chlorophyll
Torch	Sunlight

Misconceptions

This activity addresses some misconceptions about gas exchange in animals. Carbon dioxide is entering the lungs of the bird but it is not entering the bloodstream.

Process

Warm-up (5 minutes)

Psst! (see page 129). Use statements about plant nutrition and the carbon cycle.

Activity (5 minutes for the play, plus 15 minutes rehearsal time – total activity time 20 minutes)

Note: The play can be carried out with a minimum of two students but up to ten can be given parts to play.

Outline

This drama is based on the writing of Primo Levi and his essay on carbon which is the final chapter in his book *The Periodic Table*.

A storyline and associated stage directions are provided. Alternatively groups can decode how they will act out the story using the available props.

Suggested script for narration and stage directions

Narrator Carbon is a special element. It is the only element that can bind itself into long stable chains without needing lots of energy. For life on Earth (the only sophisticated life on a planet we know of so far) many chemicals with long chains are required. So, carbon is the key element of living things. But its entry into the living world is not easy and follows an intricate path.

In this limestone rock there's an atom of carbon bonded to oxygen and calcium. The carbon has been stuck in a limestone cliff for hundreds of millions of years.

Show large piece of limestone.

Narrator Along comes a miner and, with her pickaxe, she breaks off the limestone and roasts it in her lime kiln.

Mime using a pick axe to chip off rock. Pick up small piece of limestone in tongs and wave in direction of Bunsen flame (do not heat).

Narrator Still clinging to two oxygen atoms, off goes the carbon atom as part of a molecule of carbon dioxide. Now it's free from the rock to helter-skelter through the atmosphere, where it's lifted up ten kilometres.

Throw molecular model of carbon dioxide up in the air.

Narrator On its way down to Earth the carbon dioxide is inhaled by a bird, but does not enter the bird's bloodstream.

Catch the carbon dioxide model and move it towards the bird model, skeleton or picture (in Primo Levi's original writing this was a falcon).

Narrator Over the next 100 years it dissolves in and out of the oceans on three occasions.

Drop the carbon dioxide molecular model into the trough of blue water.

Narrator Then, today the amazing day arrives – the carbon dioxide enters the stoma of a leaf bumping into useless molecules such as oxygen and nitrogen on its way.

Mime this through the hole cut in the large paper leaf bumping into molecular models of oxygen and nitrogen.

Narrator But then in something in the scale of a millionth of a millimetre, in a happening that takes just the millionth of a second, using chlorophyll to activate it.

Drop the carbon dioxide molecule into the trough of green water.

Narrator The carbon is nailed by a photon of light into a carbon chain.

Flash a torch onto the carbon dioxide model in the green water.

Narrator Long or short, it doesn't matter, it is made into the chain of life. An incredible reaction with no noise, no added heat required, no smell . . . . This happens every day wherever plants are green! The beginning of photosynthesis.

Hold up molecular model of glucose.

Carbon dioxide entering the stoma of a leaf.

Differentiation

Able students can be asked to extend the drama – what happens next? In Levi's original writing the glucose travelled from the leaf to the trunk of a vine and into a grape. This bunch of grapes was used to make wine. The particular molecule of glucose was not fermented and ended up in the liver of a wine drinker – until the man who had drunk the wine chased a horse and the glucose was broken down in his thigh muscle into lactic acid, and later into carbon dioxide and water. This time the carbon dioxide became incorporated into a tree, it was eaten by an insect larva, and became part of the insect's eye, before the insect died and decayed, re-releasing the carbon atom as carbon dioxide . . . .but any number of scenarios are possible.

> **Watch out for:** The use of the Bunsen burner to model the kiln adds to the effect, but students should be given clear instructions not to heat the limestone.

Cells • Sandra Campbell

Total time 12 minutes

Aims and outcomes

- To learn that life processes are supported by the organization of cells into tissues, organs and body systems.

Location

In a gym hall, ideally in PE kit so that students can be more expressive. There are opportunities for collaboration with PE teachers in setting up and carrying out this activity. Alternatively, a clear space in a lab or classroom can be used.

Resources required

Different coloured clothing such as bibs, tabards, t-shirts or sweat shirts, including black (nuclei) and green (chloroplasts). Green balloons or balls to represent chloroplasts and rope loop or a small hoola-hoop to represent vacuole in plant cells.

A4 photomicrographs and/or diagrams of each cell type may help to stimulate students' ideas. Music and means to play it (optional).

Misconceptions

The cytoplasm is not represented in this activity and students should be made aware of this. The shape of a hoola-hoop means that it is not an ideal representation of a vacuole, so having students or rope to represent the vacuole is preferable. The misconception that any particular cell can 'morph' into any other cell could arise.

This activity may help students understand the link between a two-dimensional diagram and a three-dimensional representation. Student can readily make a three-dimensional animal half-cell by forming a circle, facing together, arms around shoulders and touching heads together around a crouching 'nucleus'.

Process

Warm-up (7 minutes)

Touch three things (see page 130).

Activity (5 minutes for the play, plus rehearsal time)

Outline

In this activity students move to represent a typical plant or animal cell and then 'morph' into a specialized cell. Particularly for the plant cells, it is good to try to differentiate between students representing different layers of cells by using different colour clothing. If this activity is carried out in the school hall students can sit or lie on the floor or on mats to make some of the cells – try to encourage them not to see this just as a standing up activity. Sperm cells can move, muscle cells can 'twitch', nerve cells can flutter their hands and feet bringing in elements of expressive dance movements. Ask students to rehearse each animal cell or each plant cell in turn. Then ask a stem cell to call out 'Specialize as a nerve cell' (or any of the other choices) to change position. You can have gentle music playing as students mime or dance.

You may want to separate your students into plant and animal cell groups. Miming animal cells is more straightforward to start with. A larger group means flexibility, but you could start with six students representing a typical animal cell and build up from there.

Instructions

	12 students	24–30 students
Typical animal cell	One student wearing a black tabard acts as the nucleus. The remainder of the students link arms to form the cell membrane	Three students wearing black tabards stand closely together as the nucleus. The remainder of students link arm to form the cell membrane
Typical plant cell	Nucleus and one student as a chloroplast. Vacuole can be represented by a loop of rope or a small hoola-hoop. Four to five students as cell membrane surrounded by four to five students arms out-stretched, hands on each other's shoulders as 'stiff' cell wall	More students can be used to represent the vacuole. Use colours to differentiate between the parts of the cell. This can be simple cloth tabards, PE bibs, school sweat shirts, sports kit, lab coats, clothing from home
Specialized animal cell – nerve cell	Facing outwards, students of the cell membrane extend their arms and legs to reach out	Facing outwards, students of the cell membrane extend their arms and legs to reach out Students represent nerve cell dendrites.
Specialized animal cell – red blood cell	Students arrange themselves into the shape of biconcave discs. Student representing nucleus leaves	Students arrange themselves into the shape of biconcave discs, Students representing nuclei leaves
Specialized animal cell – sperm cell	Small group of students surround the nucleus to represent the head of the sperm, the rest of the students form a conga-like chain to represent the tail	Small group of students surround the nuclei to represent the head of the sperm, the rest of the students form conga-like chains to represent the tails

	12 students	24–30 students
Specialized animal cell – muscle cell	The cell membrane students stretch out to form a long thin cell with the nucleus in the middle	The cell membrane students stretch out to form a long thin cell with a nucleus
Specialized plant cell – palisade cell	As a typical plant cell incorporating green balloons as chloroplasts	As a typical plant cell but more students in a green tabards or green balloons to represent chloroplasts Students represent a plant cell.
Specialized plant cell – xylem cell	As a typical plant cell but make long and thin	As a typical plant cell but make long and thin
Specialized plant cell – root hair cell	Students all sitting or lying on the floor. Any student representing chloroplasts leave. An extension of two to three students is used to represent the root hair cell	Students all sitting or lying on the floor. Any student representing chloroplasts leave. An extension of two to three students is used to represent the root hair cell Students represent root hair.

Differentiation

Most students will be able to take part in this activity which is not strenuous. If any student cannot because of physical disability they can be given a role to play as the stem cell or a reporter.

You can differentiate this activity by the amount of guidance given – students may want to choose other cells to represent. Although this activity has largely focused on the structure of the cell, students can be encouraged to use mime or dance to link the structure of the cell to its function.

With a large group and a 'nucleus' of at least four students, cell division can be acted out. The one nucleus re-forms into two and they move apart. The cell membrane re-forms separately around each nucleus.

Reed warblers and cuckoos • Sandra Campbell

Total time 35 minutes

Aims and outcomes
- To learn survival rates of prey.
- To appreciate links between variation and natural selection and that better adapted (camouflaged) individuals have improved survival and so breeding chances.

Location
A grass area in which to play the activity needs to be defined, 30m × 30m is sufficient, but it can also be done in a smaller area. Choose an area with clear markers already in place (distinctive trees, bushes, hedges, fences, pathways, etc.) or mark the area with cones. The activity can be adapted for indoor use using a piece of military/birdwatching camouflage netting which can be held above the students' heads, who then pick the wool through it. Wool can be cut in smaller sections for this and may represent caterpillars on trees, rather than worms.

Resources required
A laminated stimulus picture of a reed warbler feeding a cuckoo (optional). 'Worms' made from many pieces of differently coloured wool 3–4cm long. There should be a mixture of different colours including some dull greens and browns and some bright colours. There should be at least six worms per player – so for a class of 30 you may lay out 180 pieces of wool –15 worms in each of 12 different colours. A 'tongue' made from a piece of card with double-sided sticky tape on it. Make sure the tongue is long enough for the amount of wool you laid out. Hold back one worm in each colour for reference. If necessary, cones or tape to define the boundaries of the area where the game is to be played.

Misconceptions
Only two reed warbler parents would normally feed the cuckoo, on a variety of organisms. Not really a misconception, but it is worth asking the students to predict which colour worms will be easiest to find – some shades of green show up very readily on grass!

Process
Warm-up (5 minutes)
Fruit salad (see page 126).

Activity (30 minutes)

Outline
The activity shows the camouflage advantage of prey collected by warbler 'slave' birds to feed the parasitic cuckoo.

Instructions
1. One student (or the teacher) is allocated the role of cuckoo. The cuckoo holds the tongue. The rest of the group plays reed warblers. They gather close to the cuckoo.
2. The cuckoo shouts 'Feed me, feed me!' and the reed warblers go and find a worm (piece of coloured wool) and bring it back to the cuckoo and stick it on the tongue. Students are only allowed to collect one piece of wool at a time.
3. Wool is stuck on the tongue in order of its arrival.
4. This is then repeated four or five times; each time the reed warblers go and collect worms and bring them back to the cuckoo, adding them in order to the tongue.
5. You should find that the brightly coloured worms are collected first, and the duller greens and browns are collected last (if at all), illustrating camouflage.

Wool 'worms' placed on the model cuckoo tongue.

Note: Ensure students only collect one piece of wool at a time and set clear boundaries for the activity. If all the wool is not found explain to students that it is biodegradable.

Differentiation

If not all the wool is found, and most often it is not, this activity can be adapted to make a more quantitative activity and a bar chart constructed from results. Students who are unable to walk or bend down to pick up worms could be given the role of the cuckoo.

For a related extension activity visit: http://darwin.britishcouncil.org/activities/worms-and-birds-age-11-16 to find details of the Wellcome Trust activity looking at natural selection in action which uses spaghetti worms of different colours left out for garden birds.

Watch out for: If using a local park, check the area for dog mess.

Chemistry:
session plans for 11–14

This chapter contains the following session plans

Particle arrangements in solids, liquids and gases – going further • Ruth Amos

Total time 27 minutes

Aims and outcomes

* To understand that the particle model provides an explanation for the different physical properties and behaviour of matter.
* To learn that there is (to all intents) no space between the particles in a liquid.
* To understand that models have limitations in their ability to accurately explain abstract scientific ideas.

Location

Possible in the classroom but it's better to relocate to a hall (you could go outside but bear in mind that instructions/storyline may be more difficult to hear).

Resources required

It is very useful to make hats or headbands to identify players more clearly. So, for example, the solid particles wear headbands with 'Salma/Sammy Solid', liquid particles wear 'Lola/Leo Liquid' headbands and gaseous particles wear 'Georgy/Guido Gas' headbands. If holding hands is not appropriate for the solid particles then make short strips of paper for students to hold together.

Misconceptions

It seems that the most challenging idea for learners to fully embrace is that particles in a liquid have, to all intents, no space between them. This lasts well into the adult lives of even our best trainee teachers and is reinforced time and again through incorrect animations and particle diagrams in textbooks (the accurate 'picture' is very difficult to create in 2D). The drama may reinforce this misconception, as well as give the impression that there *is* space between the particles in a solid, because it is not possible to get the students close together enough to fully show this characteristic. Students therefore need to think particularly of their arms and hands as being the 'edges' of the particles, not just their torsos. Another possible misconception is that particles in a gas can change direction without the action of an external force. The gas particles need to keep moving in straight lines unless they 'collide' with anything/another particle. The scenario below does not accurately describe how a fizzy drink would actually freeze (i.e. Scene 1 describes the solid at the bottom of the bottle, etc. but this set-up is designed to simplify an already complex scene).

Process

Warm-up (7 minutes)

Touch three things (see page 130).

Activity (20 minutes)

Outline

The lead-in to the role play could involve students making their own hats/headbands for the action – time is needed for this. Once hats/headbands are made they can be used for different role plays.

Also, the instructions can either be read out by the teacher, or a confident student narrator, or each of the different players can be given their script of words and/or actions in advance to learn their parts in essence, then the narrator/teacher can guide as necessary and support the starting of the scenes. What follows is a story, with actions. All the actions can be preceded by, or followed up with, a discussion about the processes involved e.g. predict how the particles will change position when they move from being solid to liquid. Freeze frames are useful for this. The scenario described below is designed for students to *apply* their understanding of the arrangements of particles in solids, liquids and gases; a more simple role play of the particle arrangements in each can be run prior to the main role play described below while students *explore* the ideas initially. For example, as a warm-up, ask the students to show arrangements for only one state at a time – i.e. the solid, then the liquid, then the gas.

Instructions

Story

Narrator (setting the scene) Three friends return from a trip to the park on a hot day; feeling thirsty, one of them remembers a bottle of fizzy drink in the freezer.

Scene 1

Narrator Inside the cold freezer, a bottle of fizzy drink is waiting to be opened ... the liquid inside is half frozen.

Action: 10–12 students (wearing Salma/Sammy Solid headbands) standing close together, side by side, holding hands or holding strips of paper between their hands, inside an imaginary bottle (at the bottom). The solid particles just shiver a little on the spot. 10–12 students (with Lola/Leo Liquid headbands) standing close together – the same arrangement as the solid particles – side by side, not holding hands, inside the imaginary bottle (at the top). The liquid particles jiggle gently on the spot. Six to eight students (with Georgy/Guido Gas headbands) stand just 'above' the liquid particles, in the imaginary neck of the bottle. The gas particles jiggle a lot on the spot (carefully).

A group of solid particles.

Scene 2

Friend no. 1 I'm so hot, I really need a cool drink.

Friend no. 2 Hey, I put a bottle in the freezer the other day – should be really cool by now.

Actions: The friends come into the kitchen. Friend no. 2 opens the imaginary freezer door and guides the bottle out by opening her/his arms and directing the bottle a few paces. All the drink particles shuffle slowly and carefully, staying together as they are in the bottle, out of the freezer in the direction in which friend no. 2 guides them, using his or her arms.

Scene 3

Friend no. 1 Oh look, the drink has frozen a bit ... that's no good.

Friend no. 2 But look, don't worry, there's still some liquid at the top we can have.

Friend no. 3 Let's open it up.

Actions: Friends examining the bottle, looking at the ice, etc., walking around it. All the particles continue to stand on the spot, shivering or jiggling as in scene 1. Friend no. 3 takes hold of the imaginary bottle lid and turns it slowly to take it off.

Students wearing solid, liquid and gas head bands in the bottle with the lid about to be removed.

Scene 4

The friends   (all screech together) Oh no!

Actions: All the Georgy/Guido Gas particles shoot out of the imaginary bottle (carefully) and run, in straight lines (unless they 'collide', then they bounce off at an equal angle), out into as much space as they can.

Scene 5

Friend no. 3   What a mess ... never mind let's have that drink.

Actions: Friends no. 1 and no. 2 hold the sides of the imaginary bottle and tip it to pour the liquid drink into an imaginary cup. All the Lola/Leo Liquid particles, staying as close together as possible, move and flow around each other as they are poured out into an imaginary cup.

Scene 6

Friend no. 2   Now what do we do with the frozen bit?
Friend no. 1   Let's come back in a while – it will melt in this hot weather.

Actions: The friends wander off stage, leaving the Salma/Sammy Solid particles shivering in the bottle.

Scene 7

Narrator   About 1 hour later ...

Actions: Four to six of the Salma/Sammy Solid particles are jiggling, rather than shivering, and have let go of the hands (or paper strips) of the others. They have also swapped their headbands to Lola/Leo Liquid ones.

Friend no. 2   Hey, look at that.

Actions: The three friends come back and examine the imaginary bottle of drink, walking round it. Friends no. 2 and no. 3 pour the particles out and the four to six particles, staying as close together as possible, move and flow around each other as they are poured out into an imaginary cup. The remaining solid particles shiver as before.

Note: Make sure that students try to coordinate the 'change in state' to increase everyone's understanding of the concept. The narrator needs to be a strong character.

Differentiation

The most challenging roles are the liquid particles, the most simple roles are the gas particles and so set up the role plays accordingly. Teachers need to work hard to reinforce the 'close together' characteristics of particles in a solid, and particularly in a liquid throughout the whole role play.

> **Watch out for:** Reminders such as taking care when 'colliding' if this is considered appropriate (some classes might need a 'no contact rule').

Physical processes – soluble or insoluble/making a solution •
Ruth Amos

Total time 20 minutes

Aims and outcomes

- To understand that the particle model provides explanations for the different physical properties and behaviour of matter.
- To recognize that substances do not 'disappear' when dissolving in a solvent.
- To understand that models have limitations in their ability to accurately explain abstract scientific ideas.

Location

This is possible in the classroom but it is better to relocate to a hall (you could go outside but bear in mind that instructions/storyline may be more difficult to hear).

Resources required

It is very useful to make hats or headbands to identify players more clearly. You will need enough headbands for the following: Gold scenes: 12 solid gold particles and 12 water particles. Sugar scenes: 12 solid sugar particles and 12 water particles.

If holding hands is not appropriate for the solid particles then make short strips of paper for students to hold together. You will also need four chairs laid out in a 'kayak' formation i.e. two chairs per kayak, one in front of the other. Paddles are also needed (although these could be imaginary), together with a large bucket, a large magnifying glass, a big wooden spoon.

The characters in the gold rush story could dress in suitable hats, etc. if desired.

Misconceptions

The role play is designed to illustrate that dissolving is a physical change, as well as to explore solubility/insolubility. Students commonly think that mass is not conserved when something dissolves – i.e. it disappears.

There is also the potential for the role play to negatively reinforce the idea that particles in a liquid have, to all intents, space between them.

The role play may also give the impression that there *is* space between the particles in a solid, because it is not possible to get the students close together enough to fully show this characteristic. Students therefore need to think particularly of their arms and hands as being the 'edges' of the particles, not just their torsos.

Process

Warm-up (5 minutes)

Fruit salad (see page 126).

Activity (15 minutes)

Outline

The lead-in to the role play could involve students making their own headbands for the action – time is needed for this. Once headbands are made they can be used for different role plays.

The instructions can either be read out by the teacher, or a confident student narrator, or each of the different players can be given their script of words and/or actions in advance to learn their parts in essence, then the narrator/teacher can guide as necessary and support the starting of the scenes. What follows is a story, with actions. All the actions can be preceded by, or followed up with, a discussion about the processes involved e.g. predict how the particles will change 'position' when they become 'dissolved'. Freeze frames are useful for this. The gold scenes should be run in the same lesson as the sugar scene so soluble/insoluble comparisons can be drawn.

Instructions

The story: gold rush time in the Yukon, Canada, 1896
Scene 1

Narrator	We are back in the nineteenth century at the time of the gold rush in the Yukon valley; four gold diggers are searching for gold in the slow-running river.

Action: Two kayaks are floating along the river, the people in them paddling slowly. In the first kayak Skookum Jane/Jim and Kissme Kate/Kallam are looking down into the water, searching. In the second kayak Tagish Charlie and Patsy/Pat H. are doing the same.

Scene 2

Skookum Jane/Jim	Hey, look there's gold in that there stream.
Kissme Kate/Kallam	Yes, there! Let's stop and take a look.
Tagish Charlie	Scoop up as much as you can.

Action: The paddlers stop paddling. Patsy/Pat H. leans over the side with a big bucket and scoops up an imaginary bucketful of river water.

Scene 3 – The gold

Narrator	Inside the bucket, the gold diggers have got themselves a real haul.
One of the gold particles	(to the narrator) Hey, watch what you're doing! You are making me dizzy, you rascal.
Water particles, all together	We DO NOT mix, we DO NOT mix, we DO NOT mix . . .

Action: Narrator holds the large magnifying glass over the bucket, looks in and stirs the mixture with a big wooden spoon. 12 gold particles hold hands (or paper strips) in three groups of four to represent clumps of solid gold. The clumps of gold and 12 water particles swirl around each other, close together (carefully), as if having been stirred around in a circle. The water particles hold their hands up in front of their chests to act a little like buffers against the clumps of gold particles. All the swirling particles slow down and as they stop swirling, the clumps of gold particles sink to the bottom of the bucket with the water particles gently swirling above the clumps of gold.

Freeze frame: Stop the scene and initiate a simple discussion about the insolubility of the gold in water.

Action: The narrator counts the number of gold particles actively and out loud – they have not 'disappeared'.

The gold particles and water particles not mixing – hands held up as buffers.

Scene 4 – Back to the gold diggers

Skookum Jim   All this searching for gold is making me cold and hungry and thirsty.

Action: The gold diggers are now on the river bank out of their kayaks, looking cold, swinging their arms around their bodies.

Kissme Kate/Kallam   Let's make a brew.

Action: Tagish Charlie puts an imaginary big old kettle of water on the fire, and all gather round rubbing their hands.

Pat/Patsy H.   I hope we've got plenty sugar to put in that there tea, I'm real hungry too.

Action: Tagish Charlie then pours out four imaginary mugs of tea.

Scene 5 – The sugary tea

Narrator   The four gold diggers make their hot tea sugary sweet.

Action: Tagish Charlie spoons imaginary sugar into the mugs and stirs with the big wooden spoon. Narrator holds the large magnifying glass over the bucket and looks in. 12 sugar particles hold hands (or paper strips) in three groups of four to represent clumps of solid sugar. The clumps of sugar and 12 water particles swirl around each other (carefully), as if having been stirred around in a circle.

Water particles   We DO mix, we DO mix, we DO mix . . .

Action: The water particles hold their hands down by their sides, moving around the gold particles as close together as they can; as they do so, the sugar particles drop hands (strips of paper) and the water particles and sugar particles weave round each other (carefully).

Freeze frame: Stop the scene and discuss the solubility of the sugar in water.

Action: The narrator counts the number of sugar particles actively and out loud to emphasize that they have not 'disappeared'.

The sugar and water particles mixing.

Note: Make sure that students try to coordinate the 'changes' to increase everyone's understanding of the concept. The narrator needs to be a strong character.

Differentiation

The sugar scene should be run immediately after the gold scenes such that the gold scenes players holding their final freeze frame, or certainly re-form it (Scene 3), alongside the final sugar scene (Scene 5). Discussions of the limitations of this role play model are definitely needed; it's difficult to portray the solid gold and the solid sugar accurately, as well as the likelihood of reinforcing the space/no space misconceptions inherent in a role play about particle arrangements in liquids and solids.

There are some good informative and some interactive websites about the Yukon (Klondike) Gold Rush which might be interesting to use before/after the role play. The Gold Rush was triggered in 1897 after the Skookum party discovered gold in 1896 – there are some good cross-curricular links here with humanities:

http://www.virtualmuseum.ca/Exhibitions/Klondike/English/main.html
http://www.questconnect.org/ak_klondike.htm

Watch out for: Remind students to take care when the particles are swirling around each other.

Evaporation and condensation • Ruth Amos

Total time 20 minutes

Aims and outcomes

- To understand that the particle model provides an explanation for the different physical properties and behaviour of matter.
- To understand that gaseous particles travel in straight lines unless acted upon by a force in another direction.
- To understand that models have limitations in their ability to accurately explain abstract scientific ideas.

Location

This is possible in the classroom but it is better to relocate to a hall (you could go outside but bear in mind that instructions/storyline may be more difficult to hear).

Resources required

Six thick pieces of A4 card (for the wind), a long sheet of aluminium foil and a torch for the sun. No other essential equipment is needed but it is possible to make stickers saying 'wind' or 'water molecule' or 'sun', or to make hats or head bands to identify players more clearly.

Misconceptions

Students might think that mass is not conserved and that evaporating molecules 'waft' around in multiple directions, rather than only change direction when hit by another molecule or hit a surface.

Process

Warm-up (5 minutes)

Fruit salad (see page 126).

Activity (15 minutes)

Outline

The lead-in to the role play could involve students making their own hats or stickers for the action although additional time would be needed for this.

The instructions can either be read out by the teacher or a confident student narrator, or each of the different players can be given their script of actions in advance to learn their parts in essence, then the narrator/teacher can guide as necessary and support the starting of the scenes. What follows is a story, with actions. All the actions can be preceded by, or followed up with, a discussion about the processes involved e.g. predict which direction(s) the water molecule will move in when they evaporate. Freeze frames are useful for this.

Instructions

Story
Scene 1

Narrator   There is puddle of sleepy water molecules moving gently from side to side. One or two of the molecules are a bit wakeful.

Action: 10–12 students standing close together, side by side, swaying or flowing slightly. One or two molecules break free and vaporize and start to move more quickly, in straight lines, around the room.

Scene 2

Narrator   A gentle breeze begins to blow across the puddle from one side.

Action: The narrator opens the window – this could be an imaginary window. Six students flap A4 cards marked 'wind' at the puddle gently. A few puddle molecules begin to move more and escape from the puddle, in straight lines, until they collide with one another gently, or gently with a surface when they change direction. The narrator closes the window and the wind stops blowing. Already vaporized puddle molecules remain as vapour but molecules move more slowly.

The wind blowing at the water molecules in the puddle.

Scene 3

Narrator   The sun comes out.

Action: One student, positioned somewhere visible to all, turns on her/his torch and shines it at the remaining puddle molecules. A few more puddle molecules begin to move more and escape from the puddle, in straight lines, until they collide with one another gently, or gently with a surface when they change direction. Finally all the puddle molecules are now vapour.

Scene 4

Narrator   A large, icy wall appears.

Action: The sun student switches off the torch; the molecules move more slowly, etc. Three students hold the aluminium sheet across one side of the stage. The students make the sheet 'shiver' to represent a cold surface. As each water molecule eventually hits the icy wall, they 'condense' by slowing down as they rebound and all go to re-form the puddle.

Note: Make sure that students try to coordinate the 'change in state' to increase everyone's understanding of the concept. The narrator needs to be a strong character.

Water vapour students collide with the aluminium sheet. A few other students, as liquid water, are under the sheet, having condensed to form a puddle.

Differentiation

There could be specific roles for certain students e.g. by asking an able student to role play the most energetic molecule and explain to the class why their actions model such a molecule.

> **Watch out for:** Reminders such as taking care when 'colliding' if this is considered appropriate (some classes might need a 'no contact rule').

Physical and chemical processes – burning a candle •
Ruth Amos

Total time 25 minutes

Aims and outcomes

- To understand that the particle model provides an explanation for the different physical properties and behaviour of matter.
- To understand that elements consist of atoms that combine together in chemical reactions to form compounds.

Location

This is possible in the classroom but it is better to relocate to a hall (you could go outside but bear in mind that instructions/storyline may be more difficult to hear).

Resources required

It is very useful to make hats or headbands to identify players more clearly. You will need enough headbands for the following: 24 solid wax particles, ten wax particles, six gas wax particles, three hydrocarbon molecules – carbon, three hydrocarbon molecule – hydrogen, ten oxygen molecules, six carbon dioxide molecules, six water molecules. If holding hands is not appropriate for the solid wax particles then make short strips of paper for students to hold together. You will also need a large match and match box (which could be real or a model), a length of rope (or thick string if rope is not available) to act at the wick, a yellow flame drawn on card and a large magnifying glass.

Misconceptions

The main purpose of the role play is to illustrate that there are physical *and* chemical changes happening when you set a candle alight. Some students may have difficulty in separating the two kinds of process and think that mass is not conserved particularly in the combustion scenario. Some students may think that it is only the wick that burns away in a candle, not the fuel. In this role play, the wick does not burn away at all!

There is also the potential for the role play to negatively reinforce the idea that particles in a liquid have, to all intents, space between them (see page 46).

The role play may also give the impression that there *is* space between the particles in a solid, because it is not possible to get the students close together enough to fully show this characteristic. Students therefore need to think particularly of their arms and hands as being the 'edges' of the particles, not just their torsos. Another possible misconception to be aware of is some students believe that particles in a gas can change direction without the action of an external force. The 'gas' particles need to keep moving in straight lines *unless* they 'collide' with anything/another particle.

Process
Warm-up (5 minutes)
Keepy uppy (see page 128).

Activity (20 minutes)

Outline
The lead-in to the role play could involve students making their own hats/headbands for the action – time will be needed for this. Once hats/headbands are made they can be used for different role plays.

Also, the instructions can either be read out by the teacher, or a confident student narrator, or each of the different players can be given their script of words and/or actions in advance to learn their parts in essence, then the narrator/teacher can guide as necessary and support the starting of the scenes. What follows is a story, with actions. All the actions can be preceded by, or followed up with, a discussion about the processes involved e.g. predict how the particles will change position when they move from being solid to liquid. Freeze frames are useful for this, and a couple of these are suggested below. The candle-melting phase and the candle-burning phase need to be run separately to try to reinforce the physical and chemical natures of what is going on.

Story 1 – The melting candle

Scene 1

Narrator   On a dark winter's night, a candle is lit . . .

Actions: 12 students, wearing solid wax headbands, stand in a line, two by two, holding hands, (or holding strips of paper between them) close together, shivering on the spot. In between each two by two pair, the candle wick runs through the centre of the candle (held in one hand by one of each pair).

The narrator strikes the match and holds it carefully near the top end of the wick (note: do not actually light the candle).

One solid wax particle at the top end holds up the yellow card flame.

The melting candle.

Scene 2

Narrator   As the candle wax warms up, it starts to melt.

Actions: The four solid wax particles at the top of the candle change their headbands for liquid wax headbands and begin to jiggle a lot and let go of each other's hands (or strips of paper). They need to keep hold of their solid wax headbands. Slowly they move down past the outside of the other eight solid wax particles as if they are dripping down the outside of the candle. Particles should stay as close together as possible. The wick will just have to hang down, and the yellow flame gets passed down the candle! Once they get to the bottom end of the candle, they hold hands with one of the solid wax particles, i.e. join on again as they have resolidified and become 'solid' drips. They swap their liquid wax headbands.

Freeze frame: Freeze the scene and get the audience to explain what has happened in terms of physical changes.

Introduce Story 2 – ask the students to explain what will happen now if the candle wax actually starts to burn.

Story 2 – The burning candle

Scene 1

Narrator   On a dark winter's night, a candle is lit . . .

Actions: 12 students, wearing solid wax headbands stand in a line, two by two, holding hands, (or holding strips of paper between them) close together, shivering on the spot. In between each two by two pair, the candle wick runs through the centre of the candle (held in one hand by one of each pair). Another student strikes the match and holds it carefully near the top end of the wick (note: do not actually light the candle). One solid wax particle at the top end holds up the yellow flame.

Scene 2

Narrator   As the candle wax warms up, it starts to melt . . . and then as it gets hotter.

Actions: The six solid wax particles at the top of the candle change their headbands for liquid wax headbands and begin to jiggle a lot and let go of each other's hands (strips of paper), but they do not put the liquid wax headbands on; they immediately swap them for gas headbands and put those on. The gas particles keep jiggling but for the purposes of Scene 3 below, do not fly off across the room. The yellow candle flame is held by one of the remaining solid wax particles at the top of the candle. The wick will just have to hang down.

Freeze frame: Ask the students what will happen next, as the wax starts to burn.

Set the scene by asking the audience to imagine that they can now see the molecules of which the wax is made up.

Actions: Hold up a big magnifying glass to the six gas wax particles; get three of them to swap their headbands for a hydrocarbon molecule – carbon headband and three to swap for a hydrocarbon molecule – hydrogen headband. Ten oxygen molecules enter the scene from the other side of the room, moving quickly but carefully in straight lines. Three of the oxygen molecules are holding (out of sight) two carbon dioxide headbands and three are holding two water molecule headbands. The other four hold nothing.

Scene 3

Narrator   The candle is burning really well.

Actions: The six gaseous hydrocarbon molecules swirl about in straight lines just above the top of the candle, and three of them collide (gently) with three oxygen molecules.

Three of the oxygen molecules swap their headbands for a carbon dioxide molecule headband and they give three of the hydrocarbon molecule – carbons a carbon dioxide molecule headband, which they then swap for their own. The six new carbon dioxide molecules then fly off as gas particles in straight lines across the room (carefully). Then another three oxygen molecules collide with the other three hydrocarbon – hydrogen molecules and swap their headbands for a water molecule headband and give the other three hydrocarbon molecules – hydrogen each a water molecule headband which they swap for their own. The six new water molecules fly off as gas particle in straight lines across the room (carefully). There are four spare oxygen molecules flying about too.

Note: Make sure that students try to coordinate the 'change in state' to increase everyone's understanding of the concept. The narrator needs to be a strong character.

Freeze frame: Freeze the scene and ask students to explain what has happened in the chemical process. Highlight the differences between this and the physical melting of the wax in Story 1, etc.

The hydrocarbon molecules C and H colliding with oxygen.

Differentiation

Several aspects of the role play could be emphasized, or left out, to achieve different depths in explanation and understanding. Story 2 could be run immediately after Story 1 such that the players in Story 1 hold their final freeze frame, or certainly re-form it (Scene 2), as the final physical/chemical changes discussions take place. Discussions of the limitations of this role play model are definitely needed; discuss what would happen to the wick in reality, for example.

For higher achieving students (age 14) an attempt at balancing the equation for the combustion reaction could be made (perhaps with pentane as the hydrocarbon; while it is not a solid, there would be a manageable number of molecules to deal with). However, the approach above has been to disregard the issue of 'balancing' as it is not easy in this scenario. For lower achieving students the whole role play might be simplified, perhaps by reducing the number of molecules taking part.

> **Watch out for:** If using a real match, ensure that students do not actually light the rope/string of the wick. Reminders such as taking care when 'colliding' if this is considered appropriate (some classes might need a 'no contact rule').

The rock cycle • Chris Otter

Total time 50 minutes

Aims and outcomes

- To recall the different types of weathering that occurs in rocks.
- To appreciate how fossils form in sedimentary rocks and what happens to them as these rocks change form.
- To demonstrate an understanding of how the main rock types form and how they interconvert.

Location

The classroom.

Resources required

Lining paper (cheap and easy to get hold of from DIY stores and decorators' merchants), coloured felt tipped pens/paints, A3 sheets of paper and black marker pens.

Misconceptions

Some students may think that only weather causes weathering and that because they generally think of rocks as heavy, they'll consider small rock fragments to be stones rather than rocks. Some students may believe that all sedimentary rocks form under water, and that the oldest sedimentary rocks are the hardest and that fossils are only found in sedimentary rock and that these are preserved plant or animal.

Process

Warm-up (5 minutes)

Fruit salad (see page 126).

Activity (45 minutes)

Outline

Individual groups of students will produce animations of the formation of one of the three main rock groups i.e. sedimentary, igneous and metamorphic. The groups then come together to demonstrate the rock cycle.

1. Assign students into groups of four or five called sedimentary, metamorphic and igneous. Ensure there are the same number of groups for each rock type.
2. Students discuss the key scientific points that need to be included in their animation demonstrating how their rock type is formed e.g. weathering, sedimentation, cementation, application of high pressure, melting, crystal formation, and list these on flip chart paper, grouping them in to the three rock types.
3. Groups are given 10 minutes to devise their presentations.
4. Each group demonstrates their rock formation animation to the whole class, with their key words displayed beside them. They stop their human animation at key points and add labels written on the A3 paper.
5. Members of the class provide feedback to each group on how their animation could be improved.
6. Each group has 5 minutes to discuss and implement improvements.
7. On the floor of the classroom place a large template of the rock cycle drawn onto lining paper. You can find suitable templates in most science text books. Three groups (one sedimentary, one metamorphic and one igneous) come together to make one new group. This new large group now repeat their three animations. The sedimentary group perform their animation first. As soon as the sedimentary rock group has 'formed' the metamorphic group take up their positions and once their rock type has 'formed', the igneous group do their animation to produce an igneous rock. The sedimentary group take over to show how igneous rocks are converted to sedimentary rocks. Take care to have all groups not involved in the animation be still, watching the group that is performing their animation.

Metamorphic rock under heat and pressure.

Note: Ensure students are using the correct scientific vocabulary.

Differentiation

* Intrusive and extrusive igneous rocks could be produced.
* Students who are less willing to take part in the animations might be tasked with drawing the floor template or making signs to add to the final rock cycle.
* Include fossil formation in the sedimentary rock formation and show how these can deform during the formation of metamorphic rocks.
* Ask students to add labels onto the final rock cycle naming rocks e.g. sandstone, basalt, slate. Either give them the names of the rock type to add or ask them to write their own labels to add at given points in the cycle.
* You might like to work with the art department to produce a large colourful floor plan of the rock cycle.

Watch out for: Take care with silliness, pushing, etc. while students are moving around.

Distillation • Chris Otter

Total time 20 minutes

Aims and outcomes

- To be able to explain how a mixture of liquids will separate into their individual components during distillation.

Location

The classroom or teaching room with a clear floor space.

Resources required

Chalk, A4 labels of a round-bottomed flask, a condenser and a collection flask. You may like to have an image of each of the appropriate pieces of equipment on each label. You will also need one card per student on which will be written a temperature (e.g. 58°C) with each temperature representing the boiling point of a component in the mixture. Ensure there are multiple cards for each component. A PowerPoint with an image of a thermometer that can be used to show one temperature (one slide for each of the temperatures used above) starting from room temperature.

Misconceptions

Some students may think that a clear colourless liquid is made up of only one component and/or that the temperature of a boiling mixture of liquids is the same as the vapour temperature above it.

Process

Warm-up (5 minutes)

Hand circle (see page 127).

Activity (15 minutes)

Instructions

Using chalk, draw out the outline of a distillation apparatus – round-bottomed flask, condenser and collection flask on the floor of the lab/classroom.

1. Students each select one of the temperature labels and each stands in the section of the chalk diagram labelled 'round-bottomed flask'.

Student particles sitting in the round-bottomed flask with their temperature labels.

2. On the board put up the temperature relating to room temperature. Each student is one particle in the distillation mixture. Students need to act out the movement of their particle at the given temperature i.e. in this case, room temperature.

3. On the board display the first boiling point relating to the student cards.

4. Students need to act out the particles at the given temperature. Those students with the given boiling point move out of the round-bottomed flask and up into the condenser.

5. Students in the round-bottomed flask keep moving in the flask. Those in the condenser represent turning from the gaseous to liquid state and from there they move into the collection flask.

Student particles labelled 48°C having moved into the condenser.

Once all the students representing the component with the given boiling point have entered the collection flask it is 'emptied' and the next boiling point is put up on the board.

6. Repeat steps 4 and 5 until all the particles have gone through the distillation process.

Note: Ensure students are using the correct scientific vocabulary.

Differentiation
- Add labels to show the difference in temperature of liquids and vapour.
- Use more complex mixtures, including those where boiling points of the liquids are very close to each other, introducing the need for a fractionation column.

> **Watch out for:** Take care with silliness and pushing while students are moving around.

pH scale • Chris Otter

Total time 22 minutes

Aims and outcomes
- To assign pH ranges to acid, neutral and alkali.
- To know the colours associated with universal indicator across the pH range (or, alternatively, certain key values you are interested in such as 1, 4, 7, 10 and 14).
- To be able to give examples of everyday materials that can be classified as acidic, neutral or alkaline.

Location
The classroom or teaching room with a clear floor space.

Resources required
For the whole class (i.e. one set) you will need samples of materials that you would wish students to know the pH of e.g. lemon, oven cleaner and milk. Access to information about the pH scale e.g. text books, internet.

For each group you will need A4 coloured cards, block-coloured to represent the 14 colours of the pH scale using universal indicator (or the particular values you are interested in). Alternatively you might have a range of clothing in these colours e.g. hats, scarves, sweatshirts that students have been asked to bring in and A4-size cards printed with numbers 1–14 (one card per number).

Misconceptions
Some students may believe that that universal indicator is the only pH indicator available.

Process
Warm-up (7 minutes)
Touch three things (see page 130).

Activity (15 minutes)

Instructions
1. With the whole class show the examples of materials you want them to know the pH of (lemon juice, oven cleaner, etc.).
2. Either discuss using Q&A what the pH is for each of these materials or tell them they will need to research these values.
3. Set them the task of producing a pH line for a class of students aged 10–11 who will be visiting the school.
4. Each group (of approximately six students) will be given one set of equipment.
5. Students have 10 minutes to produce a human pH line that uses the colours of universal indicator, the pH numbers associated with it and representations of each of the materials you want to be added to the pH line.
6. Typically students might place the coloured and numbered cards on the floor with the appropriate colour above it. They then act out the substance at a particular pH e.g. hold their arms up in the shape of a lemon and pull a pinched face to represent the sour taste. Remember to encourage students to think about representing all their senses.
7. Ask each group in turn to produce a freeze frame of their line and on your count bring each section of their line to life (e.g. if you call 'pH7' the student representing pH7 comes to life representing water). You then call out 'Stop' to 'freeze' the pH 7 student and select another pH value to bring that student 'to life' with their animation.

Note: Ensure students are using the correct scientific vocabulary when using acid/acidic or alkali/alkaline.

Differentiation

- Students might research the pH of a range of substances beforehand as homework and represent these on their line.
- Students might represent degree of acidity or alkalinity on their line.
- Students might use the completed line to represent neutralization e.g. represent what happens when lemon juice is added to milk of magnesia.

Watch out for: Take care with silliness and pushing while students are moving around.

Elements, mixtures and compounds • Chris Otter

Total time 22 minutes

Aims and outcomes

- To recognize that materials can be made up of one or more kinds of different particles.
- To be able to describe the type and arrangement of atoms in elements, compounds and mixtures.
- To use a particle model to explain the differences between the terms atoms, elements, compounds and mixtures.

Location

The classroom or teaching room with a clear floor space.

Resources required

Coloured sashes or bibs from the PE department; three different colours with an equal number of each.

Misconceptions

Some students can believe that elements are always mono atomic and so try to incorporate examples where the element is multi atomic e.g. P_4 or O_2. By representing chemical bonding, irrespective of the type (i.e. covalent, ionic or metallic), in the same way students might be encouraged, erroneously, to believe that bonding is the same.

Process

Warm-up (7 minutes)

Touch three things (see page 130).

Activity (15 minutes)

Instructions

1. Each student puts on a coloured bib or sash.
2. Place students in groups of approximately nine with three wearing each coloured sash.
3. Shout out 'Element'. Count down from 15 as students arrange themselves to represent elements e.g. each group is made up of atoms (represented by one student) all wearing the same coloured sash. Students with the same coloured sash might hold hands to represent molecular elements such as nitrogen or oxygen. Shout 'Freeze' and all students must stand completely still.
4. Comment on the arrangements students have made, correcting any incorrect freeze frames e.g. groups made up of students wearing a range of different coloured sashes.
5. Shout out 'Compounds'. Count down from 15 as students arrange themselves in ways that they think best represent compounds i.e. students wearing different coloured sashes need to represent the fact that they are bonded to each other. These may be in different ratios. You might wish to give specific examples e.g. sodium chloride, carbon dioxide. Shout 'Freeze' and all students must stand completely still. Comment on the arrangements students have made, correcting any incorrect freeze frames e.g. if a group consists of students 'bonded' together with only one coloured sash, this needs correcting.

Students form carbon dioxide.

6. Give different types of mixtures e.g. a mixture of elements, a mixture of compounds, a mixture of element/s and compound/s.

7. Assign each group a type of mixture they are to represent. Shout out 'Mixture'. Count down from 15 as students arrange themselves to represent the type of mixture they have been asked to represent. Shout 'Freeze' and all students must stand completely still.

8. Ask students to remember their exact positions in the freeze frame. Sit all groups but one down. Ask sitting students to decide what type of mixture is being represented. Repeat for all groups.

Note: Ensure students are using the correct scientific vocabulary.

Differentiation

- You might choose to give molecular elements (see note above).
- You might wish to give specific examples of compounds e.g. sodium chloride, carbon dioxide for students to model.
- You may like to allocate sash colours e.g. yellow is sulphur, black is carbon, and ask students to make their own compounds.

Watch out for: Take care with silliness and pushing while students are moving around and ensure sashes are not wound around students' necks.

5

Chemistry: session plans for 14–16

This chapter contains the following session plans

Balancing equations – the Haber process • Ruth Amos

Total time 20 minutes

Aims and outcomes

- To know that in a chemical reaction reactants are changed into products.
- To recognize the reactants and products in a word equation.
- To construct word equations given the reactants and products.
- To construct balanced symbol equations given the names of the reactants and products.
- To recognize that chemical bonds 'hold together' atoms in molecules.

Location

This is possible in the classroom but it is better to relocate to a hall (you could go outside but bear in mind that instructions/storyline may be more difficult to hear).

Resources required

Plenty of small rectangular pieces of white paper approximately 15×4 cm^2 (to act as bonds between 'elements'), several A4 cards in different colours for students (or the teacher beforehand) to make band hats with element symbols on them (i.e. a square piece of card about 12×12 cm^2 upon which the symbol 'H' or 'N' or 'Cl' is written very large and clear, fastened with a staple to a card band which the 'element' wears on her/his head (the band is stapled at the back once size is right). A box of matches (this could be an exaggerated size) with red-headed stick inside representing the match, a big picture/drawing of a red flame (for the hydrogen/nitrogen reaction), a big picture/drawing of a pressure gauge (for the hydrogen/nitrogen reaction) and two large card arrows.

Misconceptions

In a typical balanced equation, the chemical reaction appears to be static, which is not true in reality, but is a good starting point. The bits of paper representing bonds mean that something actually exists like sticks in a model. If students do not read the pre-story instructions below carefully they might start to assign roles for oxygen molecules, etc. straightaway, ignoring the need for atoms and bonds between them, thereby revealing a possible misconception about the nature of molecules.

Process

Warm-up (5 minutes)

Keepy uppy (see page 128)

Activity (15 minutes)

Outline

The lead-in to the role play could involve students making their own hats for the action – time will be needed for this. Also, to model the sense that conservation of mass is important, students could be asked to balance on a low-level see-saw (a sturdy plank of wood, with a low pivot like a small tree or symmetrical tree branch) and to explore how they can get the see-saw to balance (this might be better for Year 11, and needs a good risk assessment).

Also, the instructions can either be read out by the teacher, or a confident student narrator, or each of the different players can be given their script of actions in advance to learn their parts in essence, then the narrator/teacher can guide as necessary and support the starting of the scenes. What follows is a story, with actions. All the actions can be preceded by a discussion about the processes involved e.g. what happens when reactant molecules start to bump into one another. The two scenes show two different reactions taking place.

Instructions

Story 1 – The reaction between hydrogen and oxygen to produce water

Pre-story: Two hydrogen molecules and one oxygen molecule are needed (six students) holding 'bonds' to join them and band hats to identify them as H or O atoms. Students need to practise having the right number of pieces of paper to make new bonds in the product molecules. For the freeze frame at the end, a further two hydrogen and one oxygen molecules are needed (six more students with hats and bonds).

Narrator   Hydrogen and oxygen molecules are leaking into the lab/hall and starting to mingle with one another.

Action: Molecules swirl around each other gently, occasionally bumping into one another but just bouncing off 10–12 students standing close together, side by side, swaying or flowing slightly.

Narrator   Unaware of the danger, a passing chemistry teacher strikes a match.

Action: Chemistry teacher strikes a match in a dramatic fashion.

Narrator   Boom! A huge explosion occurs but on a tiny, tiny scale, the hydrogen and oxygen molecules are just reacting with one another.

Action: Hydrogen molecules break bonds – one H holds on to piece of paper; oxygen molecules break bonds – one holds on to piece of paper; two H atoms join to one O atom each on opposite sides, making sure a piece of paper is there for each new O–H bond (more paper is needed). There will be two new H_2O molecules made.

Freeze frame
Narrator   Here is the balanced equation for the reaction between hydrogen and oxygen.

Action: The extra two hydrogen molecules and one oxygen molecule line up to the left of the two water molecules. Another student holds the large arrow in between reactants and product molecules pointing from left to right.

Story 2 – The reaction between nitrogen and hydrogen to produce ammonia (Haber process)

Pre-story: Three hydrogen molecules and one nitrogen molecule are needed (eight students) holding 'bonds' to join them and band hats to identify them as H or N atoms. Students need to practise having the right number of pieces of paper to make new bonds in the product molecules. For the freeze frame at the end, a further three hydrogen and one nitrogen molecules are needed (eight more students with hats and bonds).

Narrator   Hydrogen and nitrogen molecules are mingling with one another in a big, steel container.

Action: Molecules swirl around each other gently, occasionally bumping into one another but just bouncing off.

Narrator   The chemical engineer turns up the heat and turns up the pressure.

Action: A student wearing a lab coat and safety goggles on comes along and waves the flame and pressure gauge at the molecules in a dramatic fashion.

Narrator   Molecules of ammonia are produced slowly, which float off (or if the pressure is great enough settle down as a liquid).

Action: Hydrogen molecules 'break bonds' – one H holds on to piece of paper; nitrogen molecules 'break bonds' – one N holds on to piece of paper; three H atoms join to one N atom on opposite sides, making sure a piece of paper is there for each new N–H 'bond' (more paper is needed). There will be two new NH_3 molecules made.

Freeze frame

Narrator   Here is the balanced equation for the reaction between hydrogen and nitrogen.

Action: The extra three hydrogen molecules and one nitrogen molecule line up to the left of the two ammonia molecules. Another student holds the large arrow in between reactants and product molecules pointing from left to right.

Note: Make sure that students are all ready to present their balanced equations at the end of the story – they may forget this purpose in the middle of the action!

Hydrogen and nitrogen molecules mingling.

Molecules of ammonia as produced slowly.

Differentiation

If students have already covered double bonds, then the oxygen molecule could hold two pieces of paper; likewise the nitrogen molecule could hold three pieces with a bit of effort, but again this might be more useful for students aged 15–16. Also more students could be involved in a whole-class setting if the reaction was 'continuous' but again this is more appropriate for the Haber process itself than for learning about balanced equations.

Watch out for: Reminders such as taking care when 'colliding' if this is considered appropriate (some classes might need a 'no contact rule'). If the see-saw is used, no feet to be placed underneath, care to be taken while trying to achieve balance and no jumping off suddenly. The teacher needs to control the on/off movement of atoms.

Environmental chemistry – carbon dioxide in the dock ●
Ruth Amos

Total time 120 minutes

Aims and outcomes
- To consider how and why decisions about science and technology are made, including those that raise ethical issues, and about the social, economic and environmental effects of such decisions.
- To explore the evidence for carbon dioxide's impact on climate change.
- To examine reasons for and against the UK government trying to reach its voluntary CO_2 reduction target of 80 per cent from 1990 levels by 2050.
- To distinguish between scientific, environmental, social and economic evidence when constructing an argument.
- To construct arguments to justify their position with respect to the need for reducing carbon dioxide emissions.

Location
In the classroom with furniture arranged so that students can work in groups of three as well as take part in whole-class discussions.

Resources required

Enough sets of the 'Carbon dioxide in the dock' evidence cards for the whole class to work with them in groups of three (so about 10–11 sets). Evidence cards to be colour coded to organize the groups; they should be laminated and cut up beforehand and be ready in individual envelopes. Student instruction sheet (see below) and evidence sheet A, B and C for each group and the teacher instruction sheet all of which can be found on the companion website.

Misconceptions
Over the past decade or so, there has been a lot of rhetoric about climate change and, because the evidence for changes in the composition of the Earth's lower atmosphere is constantly being questioned, revised and reviewed, it is possible for a great deal of confusion to arise. Debates about climate change therefore present students with opportunities to consider the tentative nature of scientific evidence and to develop argumentation skills. Students are often confused between the effects of increasing carbon dioxide levels (the greenhouse effect) in the lower atmosphere (air, or lower troposphere) and the effects of ozone depletion in the upper atmosphere (lower stratosphere). In addition, there are concerns that low-level ozone is increasing and ozone itself is a greenhouse gas. Students may therefore be confused about what each effect actually is, and muddle which gas does what at different levels in the atmosphere. The role play argumentation and debate will help students make progress with such ideas, or possibly reinforce misconceptions if students argue skilfully for inaccurate 'evidence'/definitions. In addition, in terms of students' abilities to put together a convincing argument about any environmental issue, each evidence card has the potential to be taken at face value without students thinking about what is not being said. Teachers need to think about the unsaid evidence to ensure that students are prompted to think about counter-arguments and rebuttals.

Process
Warm-up (10 minutes at the start of both lessons i.e. 20 minutes in total)
Two truths and one lie (see page 131).

Activity (50 minutes for the initial argumentation activity in small groups and 50 minutes for the debate i.e. to run over two lessons. Total activity time 100 minutes)

Outline
Setting the scene: if possible, set the room into small group discussion mode – tables/benches around which students can discuss effectively in groups of three and then combine with another group to make larger groups of six.

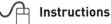

Instructions

It is the year 2010 and we are 40 years away from the deadline (2050) agreed at the Copenhagen Climate Change Conference, attended by 192 nations in December 2009, for countries across the world to reduce emissions of greenhouse gases. This is a crucial attempt to prevent the predicted average global temperature rising by more than 2°C.

Phase 1: Students engage in argumentation

You are a group of three scientific experts advising the UK government on the need to look at the impacts of reducing 'greenhouse gases' in our atmosphere. The UK government took a very forward-thinking step at the Copenhagen reduction pledge. Countries were asked to set their own targets and the UK government set an extremely ambitious target of 80 per cent reduction in carbon emissions by 2050. However, since that decision, there has been a change in government and there is a sense that the politicians are becoming nervous about the implications of such a huge reduction for people's lifestyles. Will they stick to this voluntary pledge for emission reduction or will they bottle out?

   Your task: You have to construct an argument for the government (Department for Energy and Climate Change, DECC), putting forward the positions for or against continuing with the 80 per cent reduction in carbon emissions target. You will work as a group of three initially. Listen carefully to the instructions, some of which are summarised below; other material is on the companion website.

1. Before you examine the evidence on the evidence cards, try to think of some important reasons/evidence for trying to reduce, or not trying to reduce, the levels of carbon dioxide in the Earth's atmosphere; write down three if you can.
2. Examine the evidence gathered, on the evidence cards in your envelope, about the possible causes and effects of climate change and so on.
3. Divide up the evidence cards between you. Decide in your group how to build your argument. Discuss what is meant by 'climate change'.
4. Decide who is doing what. Perhaps one of you selects all the evidence for carbon emission reduction and someone else selects the evidence against carbon emission reduction; the third person could be the writer, recording your decisions and the building of your arguments. Or you could divide all the evidence up randomly first between you and then everyone decides on the pros and cons of some of the evidence. Your teacher may assign you the for or against position. Do not let that position prevent you from putting together arguments for both sides of the debate because you need to anticipate what your opponents will say to try to win their case.
5. Record the start of your argument on evidence sheet A.
6. Think about the following questions:
   - Where do you agree; disagree?
   - Which evidence is the strongest you have chosen for and against keeping to the 80 per cent reduction in carbon emissions by 2050 target? Which evidence is the most convincing to you?
   - Now adopt the position in the argument indicated on the back of your evidence cards. In other words, either for or against and fully prepare your final argument to put to the other small group you will join soon.
7. Also, using evidence sheet B, sort your evidence into 'scientific', 'environmental', 'social' or 'economic' and see which seems to be the strongest – perhaps use different colours to show the different types of evidence. Are you as a group being swayed to one particular kind of evidence? Are you thinking carefully about the scientific and environmental evidence?
8. When instructed you will join another group of three and try to persuade them that your arguments for or against keeping to the 80 per cent reduction in carbon emissions by 2050 target are good arguments.
9. Select a spokesperson to present your case.
10. In your team of six, try to reach agreement about the strongest arguments for and against

that you have, and prepare a short presentation, choosing a spokesperson, to give your overall decision to DECC at the end of this session. In other words, you now all have to decide whether the UK government should stick to the 80 per cent carbon emission reduction by 2050 target or not, based on the evidence you have discussed today.

11. Write out your own final argument, using evidence sheet C to help you.

Phase 2: Presentation of students' arguments – the whole-class presentation

There are a number of ways the final positions of each group of six can be presented. Each group can post up evidence card C on the walls and, in a controlled manner, students can walk around and look at the different arguments. Alternatively, each group could select a spokesperson to present their argument to the whole class.

Phase 3: Final plenary discussions

Draw out examples of evidence that were weak, strong and whether groups managed to persuade/convince/change each other's minds and so forth.

Note: Teachers need to think through how to encourage taking the against position in terms of countering the evidence for. All the evidence comes from bona fide sources: students may not want to believe some of the evidence but ensure that they are analysing it carefully rather than dismissing it quickly.

Useful websites include:

Friends of the Earth www.foe.co.uk

Young People's Trust for the Environment www.ypte.org.uk

Differentiation

Higher achieving students need to be encouraged to build arguments which include counter-argument and rebuttals. Simpler arguments based upon looking for pros and cons can be framed, modelled and encouraged for lower achieving students.

Sustainable development – the World Games 2040 • Ruth Amos

Total time 20 minutes

Aims and outcomes

- To consider how and why decisions about science and technology are made, including those that raise ethical issues, and about the social, economic and environmental effects of such decisions.
- To explore the nature of materials being used to construct a World Athletics Games (perhaps akin to the 2012 London Olympics/Paralypmics).
- To recognize the environmental impacts that such a project may have.
- To distinguish between scientific, environmental, social and economic evidence when constructing an argument.
- To construct arguments to justify their position with respect to the progress of the building of the World Games venue from an environmental impact perspective.

Location

In the classroom with furniture arranged so that students can work in groups of three as well as take part in whole-class discussions.

Resources required

Enough sets of the 2040 World Games evidence cards for the whole class to work with them in groups of three (so 10–11 sets). Evidence cards to be colour coded to organize the groups and should be laminated and cut up beforehand and be ready in individual envelopes. Student instruction sheet (see below) and evidence sheets A, B and C for each group and the teacher instruction sheet. Note: All these materials are available on the companion website.

Misconceptions

Students may have an everyday understanding of the term 'sustainable development' so this activity is a good opportunity to focus on scientific issues therein. Debates present students with opportunities to consider the tentative nature of scientific evidence and to develop argumentation skills. The role play argumentation and debate will help students make progress with ideas, or possibly reinforce misconceptions if students argue skilfully for inaccurate 'evidence'/definitions. In addition, in terms of students' abilities to put together a convincing argument about any environmental issue, each evidence card has the potential to be taken at face value without students thinking about what is not being said. Teachers need to think about the unsaid evidence to ensure that students are prompted to think about counter-arguments and rebuttals.

Process

Warm-up (5 minutes)

Keepy uppy (see page 128).

Activity (15 minutes)

Outline

Setting the scene: If possible, set the room into small group discussion mode – tables/benches around which students can discuss effectively in groups of three and then combine with another group to make larger groups of six.

Instructions

It is the year 2038 and we are two years away from the 2040 World Games Park. Construction is now well underway and you are trying to decide whether the World Games Development Agency (WGDA) are committed to sustainable development. Just how environmentally friendly is all the building? Is it really justifiable to spend all that money (about £20 billion) for an event that will only last about four weeks?

Phase 1: Students engage in argumentation

You are a group of three scientific advisors reporting to the Government (Department for Culture, Media and Sport, DCMS).

Your task: you have to construct an argument for the DCMS putting forward the positions for or against whether the World Games Park is being built in a sustainable way. You will work as a group of three initially. Listen carefully to the instructions, some of which are summarised below.

1. Before you examine the evidence on the evidence cards, try to think of some important reasons/evidence which might show whether the Park is being built sustainably; write down three if you can.

2. Examine the evidence gathered, on the evidence cards in your envelope, about the ways in which the Park is being built; explore some of the impacts on local people and on the environment.

3. Divide up the evidence cards between you; decide in your group how to build your arguments. Discuss what is meant by 'sustainable development'.

4. Decide who is doing what. Perhaps one of you selects all the evidence for the Park being built in a sustainable way and someone else selects the evidence against; the third person could be the writer, recording your decisions and the building of your arguments. Or you could divide all the evidence up randomly first between you and then everyone decide on the pros and cons of some of the evidence. Your teacher may assign you the for or against position. Do not let that position prevent you from putting together arguments for both sides of the debate because you need to anticipate what your opponents will inevitably say to try to win their case.

5. Record the start of your argument on evidence sheet A.

6. Think about the following questions:
   - Where do you agree/disagree?
   - Which evidence is the strongest you have chosen for and against whether the 2040 World Games Park is being built in a sustainable way? Which evidence is the most convincing to you?
   - If you are being asked by your teacher to adopt a particular position in the argument 'for' or 'against', focus on that now and fully prepare your final argument to put to the other small group you will join soon.

7. Also, using evidence sheet B, sort your evidence into 'scientific', 'environmental', 'social' or 'economic' and see which seems to be the strongest – perhaps use different colours to show the different types of evidence. Are you as a group being swayed to one particular kind of evidence? Are you thinking carefully about the scientific and environmental evidence?

8. When instructed you will join another group of three and try to persuade them that your arguments for or against whether the 2040 World Games Park is being built in a sustainable way are good arguments.

9. Select a spokesperson to present your case.

10. In your group of six try to reach agreement about the strongest arguments for and against that you have, and prepare a short presentation, choosing a spokesperson, to give your overall decision to DCMS at the end of this session. In other words, you now all have to decide whether the Park is being built in a sustainable way, or not, based on the evidence you have discussed today.

11. Write out your own final argument, using evidence sheet C to help you.

Phase 2: Presentation of students' arguments – the whole-class presentation

There are a number of ways the final positions of each group of six can be presented. Each group can post up evidence sheet C on the walls and, in a controlled manner, students can walk around and look at the different arguments. Alternatively each group could select a spokesperson to present their argument to the whole class.

Phase 3: Final plenary discussions

Draw out examples of evidence that were weak, strong and whether groups managed to persuade/convince/change each other's minds and so forth. Note: Teachers need to think through how to encourage taking the against position in terms of countering the evidence for.

All the evidence comes from bona fide sources: students may not want to believe some of the evidence but ensure that they are analysing it carefully rather than dismissing it quickly.

Useful websites

London 2012 shows the building of the London 2012 Olympic/Paralympic Games in terms of sustainable development, http://www.london2012.com

Game Monitor – a campaign group trying to unearth information that disputes the sustainable record of the London 2012 build, http://www.gamesmonitor.org.uk/

Vancouver 2010 – shows the building of the Vancouver 2010 Winter Olympic/Paralympic Games in terms of sustainability, http://www.vancouver2010.com/sustainability/

Differentiation

Higher achieving students need to be encouraged to build arguments which include counter-argument and rebuttals. Simpler arguments based upon looking for pros and cons can be framed, modelled and encouraged for lower achieving students. Reduce the number of evidence cards too, as necessary.

Electrolysis • Chris Otter

Total time 27 minutes

Aims and outcomes

- To appreciate that ionic substances need to be molten (or in solution) in order to be electrolysed.
- To describe the reactions that take place at the anode and cathode when molten sodium chloride is electrolysed.
- To write balanced equations for reactions taking place during the electrolysis of molten sodium chloride.

Location

The classroom or teaching room with a clear floor space.

Resources required

An equal number of labels marked 'Na$^+$' on one side and 'Na' on the others marked 'Cl$^-$' on one side and 'Cl' on the other. These labels need to be attached to a string loop so they can be worn as reversible badges. One large bag of M&Ms (or alternative small, multi-coloured chocolate sweets) and a large piece of cardboard labelled 'anode' and a large piece of cardboard labelled 'cathode'.

Misconceptions

Some students may think that solid ionic compounds can undergo electrolysis and/or that in an ionic lattice the ions are stationary. Likewise some students might think that only one sodium ion is reduced and one chloride ion is oxidized at a time. The omission, for the sake of simplicity, of a battery from the role play circuit might generate misconceptions about the nature of electric circuits.

Process

Warm-up (5 minutes)

Fruit salad (see page 126).

Activity (20 minutes)

Instructions

Students are going to provide a role play for the electrolysis of molten sodium chloride. Typically this activity will involve all the students in one animation.

1. Approximately two-thirds of the students arrange themselves as ionic sodium chloride in a regular alternating fashion. Sodium and chloride ions are identified by the labels they have hanging round their necks. Each chloride ion has an M&M sweet representing the electron that it will give up at the anode later on the role play. The other third of the pupils represent the wire in the circuit (see step 4 for more detail).

Students arranged as positive and negative sodium and chloride ions.

2. Students need to represent the addition of heat (e.g. sodium and chloride ions begin to vibrate more and move apart) in order to provide energy for the lattice to break up into individual ions. Once molten and the ions are moving freely, insert the anode and cathode. (Large pieces of cardboard labelled anode or cathode with the appropriate charge on them. It might be useful to write an equation for what is about to happen at each electrode if this is the only example of electrolysis you will be doing in this exercise) A student (not a chloride or a sodium ion) next to the cathode has the bag of M&Ms.

Positive ions migrating towards the cathode and negative towards the anode.

3. The chloride ions gravitate to the anode where they form a line. In turn each chloride ion gives an electron (M&M sweet) to the anode and turns their neck sign around to Cl. The Cl atom then moves away from the cathode and waits for the next Cl to be generated then links arms with them (representing Cl_2).

4. The M&M that has been given to the anode passes along a line of students (representing the wires in the circuit). The final student in the wire passes the M&M to the student representing the cathode. Sodium ions need to gravitate to the cathode where they form a line. In turn each sodium ion receives an electron (M&M sweet) from the cathode as it arrives from the anode. Each sodium ion then turns their neck sign around to Na. The Na atom then moves away from the cathode.

5. These processes are repeated for all the sodium and chloride ions.
6. Either you or the students can freeze frame and run a narration of what is happening at the different stages of the process. Students can then recall what has happened at the anode and cathode and write ion equations for what has happened at each electrode then add them together to give an overall equation for the reaction.

Note: Ensure students are using the correct scientific vocabulary.

Differentiation
- You could repeat this process for lead bromide.
- For an extra challenge try the electrolysis of brine!

> **Watch out for:** Students should not eat the sweets as they have been in the laboratory. Take care with silliness and pushing while students are moving around.

Acid/alkali neutralization • Chris Otter

Total time 25 minutes

Aims and outcomes

- To understand that all acid/alkali reactions involve the same chemistry i.e. $H^+ + OH^-$ H_2O
- To be able to write word equations for neutralization reactions.
- To be able to write ion equations for acid/alkali reactions.
- To understand the role of 'spectator ions'.

Location

The classroom or teaching room with a clear floor space.

Resources required

Cards with formula of one ion on (equal number of cards for each ion in the reaction). Ensure that there is one ion card per student.

Misconceptions

Some students may think that acids are molecular in solution and that acids neutralize alkalis, or the converse, rather than there being a process of neutralization.

Process

Warm-up (5 minutes)

Keepy uppy (see page 128).

Activity (20 minutes)

Instructions

1. Students select from cards in a beaker a card labelled 'H^+', 'Cl^-', 'Na^+' and 'OH^-' (there should equal numbers of each.) They mill around the room. On a sign from the teacher they check the card of the person closest to them.
2. When H^+ and OH^- meet, they link arms to indicate they have reacted together to produce water. Any other meeting between students does not result in a 'reaction.'
3. Repeat the above process until all the H^+ and OH^- have 'reacted' when students stop moving around.
4. The teacher then gathers the class together to write a formula equation for what has happened, emphasizing the role of spectator (unreacted) ions. Cancel spectator ions from both sides of the equation, leaving the ion equation.
5. Repeat the process, this time use H^+, NO_3^-, K^+, OH^- with the same rules applying. The final ion equation will be the same as in the first process above.

Note: Ensure students are using the correct scientific vocabulary.

Differentiation

You might like to introduce sulphuric acid (H_2SO_4) in order to introduce the idea of diprotic acids.

> **Watch out for:** Take care with silliness and pushing while students are moving around.

Addition polymerization • Chris Otter

Total time 25 minutes

Aims and outcomes

- To demonstrate an appreciation that small unsaturated molecules (monomers) react to give larger unsaturated molecule(s) (polymers).
- To understand that addition polymerization in alkenes involves breaking double bonds and reforming new single bonds.
- To be able to give the reaction conditions necessary for polymerization.

Location

The classroom or teaching room with a clear floor space

Resources required

None.

Misconceptions

Some students may think that all the monomer molecules react; this usually is *not* the case and some students can sometimes be confused about what happens to the 'free bonds' at the end of the final polymer.

Process

Warm-up (5 minutes)

Fruit salad (see page 126).

Activity (20 minutes)

Instructions

Students work in groups of eight to represent the process of polymerization of ethene to poly(ethene).

1. At any point you may wish to call out 'Freeze' and identify the main chemical points.
2. Students are asked to use their bodies to represent molecules of ethene (most usually they will have one person representing carbon and in pairs they join both hands with each other, representing a double bond between them).
3. Students then need to represent the application of high pressure (typically they will squash close to each other, maintaining the 'double bond').
4. Freeze frame.
5. On your command, students then need to represent the opening of the double bonds and forming of new single bonds. This will involve students leaving go of one pair of hands in each molecule and re-holding hands with a free hand from another molecule.
6. Students at the end of these new molecules will still have un-joined hands. On your command you could have all the groups squash closer and join un-joined hands. The whole class by now will have formed one long chain of poly(ethene).

Note: Ensure students are using the correct scientific vocabulary.

Differentiation

- Students might represent polymerization of other monomers such as tetrafluoroethene or chloroethene by representing the additional atoms such as fluorine or chlorine.
- Modelling the synthesis of poly(propene) would be challenging.
- Once a range of polymers have been 'produced' their properties could be demonstrated and linked to their use e.g. inert nature of PTFE makes it ideal for non-stick linings on pans.
- Students might represent how branching is produced in polymers.

> **Watch out for:** Take care with silliness and pushing while students are moving around.

Exothermic and endothermic reactions • Chris Otter

Total time 20 minutes

Aims and outcomes
- To be able to represent exothermic and endothermic reactions graphically.
- To be able to label these graphs using key scientific terminology.

Location
The classroom or teaching room with a clear floor space.

Resources required
One ball of string and three bamboo canes per group.

Misconceptions
Some students believe that because an exothermic reaction is one in which energy is 'lost' from the system the temperature should drop. Likewise, some students do not realize that to start many reactions energy needs to be put into a system.

Process
Warm-up (5 minutes)
Psst! (see page 129).

Activity (15 minutes)

Instructions
1. Students work in groups of five to produce human graphs of enthalpy change during exothermic and endothermic reactions.
2. Each group sets out axes for their graphs using string.
3. Students need to label their axes to represent energy and time.
4. Each group then needs to 'draw' a line graph to represent what happens in an exothermic or endothermic reaction (typically the bamboo rods represent the energies of the starting materials, intermediate phase and products and a student will walk the energy profile of the reaction).

Students leave a white line showing the energy profile of the reaction.

5. Students can be asked to represent the energy movement from system to surroundings.
6. Human labels can be used to label key scientific ideas e.g. activation energy, energy change of reaction, starting materials, products, intermediate.

Note: Ensure students are using the correct scientific vocabulary.

Differentiation
Draw human graphs for catalysed and un-catalysed reactions.

Watch out for: Take care with silliness and pushing while students are moving around.

6

Physics:
session plans for 11–14

This chapter contains the following session plans

Electricity – conservation of charge • Ian Abrahams

Total time 20 minutes

Aims and outcomes

- To make and test predictions about current readings at different points in a circuit.
- To identify and make predictions from patterns in data.

Location

In a science lab in which the tables can be moved to form the shape of an electric circuit. Alternatively, this can be done in a hall or playground where the circuit can be marked with chalk onto the floor/surface.

Resources required

Tables/benches to arrange to make a circuit (one table should be easily placed to move into and out of the circuit to act as a switch). Three large (ideally at least 1m high) cardboard letter A cut-outs made to include hands, legs and a head/face. Four small pads of paper, a large (ideally at least 1m high) cardboard letter V cut-outs made to look like a simple weighing balance (as in blind justice) with a large number 1 hanging from one branch of the V. A hat bearing a picture of an illuminated bulb, a battery-operated torch, a shoulder bag and two pieces of rope. A large sign (flip charts are ideal for this) with the word 'Battery' on it, a cardboard box and a large supply (minimum 100, ideally more) of counters. 20 (or more) balloons of the same colour (each inflated and with the word 'Electron' written on it), each balloon having a piece of string by which it can be attached to a student's button hole/belt loop. A large poster on which is written 'Not to scale'.

Misconceptions

Some students believe that charge (electric current) is used up and that this is why their parents pay for the electricity that they 'use up' in their homes. As such, many students expect that an electric current will be less after having passed through a bulb as some of that electricity has been used up to make light and heat. This activity can generate/reinforce a misconception about the relative size of electrons and the components of the circuit.

Process

Warm-up (5 minutes)

Keepy uppy (see page 128).

Activity (15 minutes)

Outline

This activity provides students with a visual model of electron flow around a circuit. It allows them to visualize electrons and distinguish electrical energy from electrons so as to appreciate that electrons are not used up. The activity also makes clear what ammeters and voltmeters measure.

Instructions

1. Allocate roles: three students are ammeters and each has a large letter A and a pad of paper. One student is a voltmeter and they have the large letter V and a pad. One student is the battery and has the battery sign and the cardboard box of counters. Two students to act as switch operators to move the 'switch table' in and out of the circuit. The remainder of the students (or as many as you want to involve) each take on the role of an electron and are given one balloon to attach to a button hole/belt loop.
2. The battery student stands on the floor next to any part of the circuit tables with their box of counters and the sign 'Battery' clearly displayed behind them.
3. The two switch students stand on the floor on either side of the switch table (which is where the teacher is best placed).
4. The bulb student, wearing a hat bearing a picture of an illuminated bulb and holding a torch as well as a shoulder bag, stands on the floor next to any part of the circuit tables.

5. The voltmeter student, with their large V sign, stands *behind* the bulb and is linked to either side of the bulb using the two ropes.

6. Of the three ammeter students, with their signs, two are standing on the table either side of the bulb and the third can be placed on a table top at any other point in the circuit.

7. The electrons, each with an attached balloon, now all get onto the table tops and spread themselves around the circuit evenly (but there should be no-one on the switch table or directly in front of the bulb).

8. Each electron is given one counter to hold.

9. The instructions are: when the switch is closed allow each electron to move around the circuit once. Each time an electron passes the battery they are given a counter. Each time an electron passes the bulb student they pass over one counter, and for each counter the bulb person flashes their torch once. Each ammeter student counts the total number of electrons (students) that pass by them on the table top circuit (each ammeter will count the same number of students). The voltmeter counts (measures) the number of counters an electron has before going into the bulb and the number on leaving, and records the difference between these two values on their pad (in each case this should be 1).

10. It is important that students move slowly to allow the ammeters and voltmeter to count carefully and to avoid pushing anyone off the table tops.

11. A large poster, on which is written 'Not to scale', is displayed prominently throughout this activity.

Note: During the activity students should be encouraged to use the words/terms 'ammeter', 'voltmeter', 'conserved' and 'energy transformation'. The meaning of these should be made clear when opportunities present themselves and be reinforced throughout the activity.

Differentiation

This task can be made more demanding by increasing the number of counters and circuit components, but take care to calculate all of the values beforehand to ensure the model produces the desired results so as to avoid reinforcing misconceptions.

Watch out for: This activity involves the students walking on the desk tops, as this serves as a strong anchorage for their recollection of the task. Because students can get excited about the idea of walking on the tables, guidance about not being silly is advised. If you feel this approach is not suitable for your class you might try drawing a circuit on the floor using chalk, which again offers a strong anchorage point. For best grip students should either be bare-footed or wearing shoes/trainers with grip – socks provide insufficient grip and can be dangerous. Students should walk slowly on the table tops at all times.

Heat – conduction • Ian Abrahams

Total time 20 minutes

Aims and outcomes
- To understand why heat passes through different materials at different rates.
- To identify and make predictions from patterns in data.

Location
Ideally in a hall with sufficient clear room for 16 students to stand, arms outstretched on each others' shoulders in a 4 × 4 arrangement with a few metres clear around them. You will also need two electric sockets and possibly a couple of extension leads, depending on the size of the hall.

Resources required
Paper balls. 16 students wearing the same colours (this could be normal white/blue school shirts or a pre-agreed colour of t-shirt). Six or more students all wearing the same colours, but this must be a *different* colour to that worn by the other 16 students (I used to use fluorescent cycling overjackets). A large poster on which is written 'Not to scale'. Two electric fans, ideally with three settings, and a flip chart.

Misconceptions
Some students believe that heat does not pass through an insulator – even though its atoms can vibrate. This activity can generate/reinforce a misconception about the relative size of nuclei and electrons and the spaces between them.

Process
Warm-up (5 minutes)
Hand circle (see page 127).

Activity (15 minutes)

Outline
This activity provides students with a visual model of conduction of heat through solids. In this way students experience that heat energy, in the form of kinetic energy, can pass through any solid but that it is, in some materials, a slow process. Students can also experience how, in conductors, the transfer of heat energy occurs much more rapidly, and that this can be understood in terms of the existence, and more rapid movement, of free electrons.

Instructions
1. Allocate roles: 16 students form a 4 × 4 (this can be made longer if you have the students) arrangement in which each student places their hands, arms outstretched, on the shoulders of the person in front of them and keep them there for the duration of the activity.

Students in the conductor place their hands, arms outstretched, on the shoulders of the person in front of them.

2. The front row are asked to hold their hands out to illustrate that if another 'object' was to come into their reach they would be able to pass on their kinetic (heat) energy to it. A student switches on the fan at the front once they have started to vibrate, to illustrate that heat has been conducted through the material.

3. Heat is applied to the four back-row students in the form of air from the fan at the back, which can be switched on when required.

4. When the back row feel the air from the fan (heat) they count to 30 before beginning to move backwards and forwards and side to side.

5. Inform the row in front of them that, although they can feel the hands moving on their shoulders, they too need to count to 30 before beginning to move backwards and forwards and side to side. The same process is repeated for each row, the intention being to generate a wave of vibration that slowly advances from one end of the 'object' to the other over a period of 2 minutes, until the whole arrangement of 16 students is vibrating. A student in the front row, when the others start to vibrate, moves forward to turn on the front fan to indicate that heat has passed through the insulator from the back fan.

A student turns on the front fan after the other students have started to vibrate.

6. A flip chart is then placed next to the arrangement with the word 'Insulator' written on it.

7. The whole process is then started afresh, using the same 30-second wait period, although this time those six or more students, dressed in a different colour (representing free electrons),

run quickly through the columns from the rear column to the front column as soon as the fan at the back is switched on.

Students, as free electrons, run through the conductor very quickly and turn on the front fan.

8. The first one through (this usually takes no more than 15 seconds) turns on the fan at the front.
9. A flip chart is then placed next to the arrangement with the word 'Conductor' written on it.
10. A large poster, on which is written 'Not to scale', is displayed prominently throughout this activity.

Note: during the activity students should be encouraged to use the words/terms 'conductor', 'insulator', 'not to scale' and 'free electrons'. The meaning of these should be made clear when opportunities present themselves and be reinforced throughout the activity.

Differentiation

This task is designed for more able students, although without the free electrons it still provides a useful basic model of conduction through solids.

> **Watch out for:** The main issue here is that students can get excited about the idea of shaking each other and/or running into one another, and so guidance about not being silly is advised. Fans should have safety covers. Electrical flex should be securely taped to the floor to avoid presenting a tripping hazard.

Reflection • Ian Abrahams

Total time 30 minutes

Aims and outcomes
* To make and test predictions about the path of light.
* To measure and record angles.
* To identify and make predictions from patterns in data.
* To investigate reflection at a plane surface.

Location
Ideally in a room where you can either turn tables on their sides to act as mirrors, or are able to use the walls to act as two abutting mirrors. Alternatively, if weather permits and suitable external walls/surfaces are available, this is a great activity for undertaking out of doors. If undertaken out of doors you can get some really great photographs of the resulting ray paths, if you can photograph the rays from a second or higher floor.

Resources required
Lab coats, clear walls and/or tables that can be put on their sides, clip boards, large protractors, two large set squares, rolls of different coloured plastic tape (ideally at least 12m long to represent coloured beams of light), metre rules (to be placed on the floor as Normal lines), Blu-tack (to affix metre rules to the floor), adhesive tape (to affix the plastic tape to the floor), large self-adhesive badges labelled 'incident ray', 'reflected ray' and 'Normal maker' for students to wear to identify their roles to others in the class.

Note: It is possible to used coloured wools in place of plastic tape but it is visually less striking.

Misconceptions
Some students believe either that light is always reflected straight back along its incident path or, alternatively, that it is reflected at any arbitrary angle. Some students also have difficulty in understanding the meaning of the term 'Normal', how and where it is drawn and the use it plays in constructing ray diagrams. Some students believe that all Normal lines need to point in the same direction.

Process
Warm-up (5 minutes)
Hand circle (see page 127).

Activity (25 minutes)

Outline
In this activity students mark out, using different coloured plastic tapes, the paths of light rays that are incident on a table top that is acting as a mirror at different angles (Note: table tops, walls, large sheets of cardboard can all be used interchangeably). At each point where an incident ray hits the table top a student, using a large set square, places a metre rule on the floor at right angles to the wall (Blu-tack can be used to keep the ruler in place) to represent the Normal line. A student, who acts as measurer, then measures the angle of incidence, from the Normal line to the ray, using a large protractor. The measured angle is written on paper and passed to a second student who, measuring again from the Normal line, ensures that the angle at which the ray is reflected is the same as the angle of incidence. Different coloured rays can then be fired at the same point on the table with the only difference being the angle of incidence, or the incident ray can be aimed at different points on the table to practise marking in the Normal line, or a combination of both. The coloured plastic tape is stuck to the floor to leave a visual record of the path of the light ray. Multiple reflections off different tables can be undertaken.

Instructions

1. Allocate roles: one student per coloured ray used; two angle measurers at every table/wall – one to measure the angle of incidence and the other to measure the angle of reflection; one student at every table to place the Normal line (metre rule) at right angles to the surface at the point at which the ray impacts the surface. If possible one student to take photographs of the resultant ray paths.

2. Often this works best if measurers are given lab coats and clip boards and I often gave the Normal marker a construction worker's hard hat.

3. Ask the first ray to stick the end of their coloured plastic tape to the floor where they start from and unrolling the tape they move towards the table. They affix (without cutting) the tape to the floor directly in front of the table. The Normal marker then places the metre rule at right angles to the table – using a large set square – at the point at which the light hits the surface and sticks it to the floor with Blu-tack.

4. The measurer then measures the angle of incidence from the Normal to the incident ray and passes this angle value on to the second measurer who ensures that the ray departs at the same angle. When the ray reaches its second table the plastic tape is adjusted until the angle of reflection, off the previous surface, is at the correct value and then the tape is affixed in front of the second surface and the whole process can then be repeated.

Students place the Normal line and measure the angle of incidence and reflection.

Note: During the activity students should be encouraged to use the words/terms 'incident', 'reflected', 'angle of incidence', 'angle of reflection' and 'Normal'. The meaning of these should be made clear when opportunities present themselves and be reinforced throughout the activity.

Differentiation

For more able students and/or small groups tables can be positioned around the room so that only a specific initial angle of incidence, that they need to discover, will enable the ray to be multiply reflected from all of the tables to arrive at a specific end point. The activity can be made less demanding by restricting it to one table/wall with the students simply ensuring that for every measured angle of incidence the associated angle of reflection is the same.

Watch out for: The main issue here is that students can get excited about the idea of running into tables and/or walls, and guidance about not being silly is advised. If many rays are used, point out the need not to trip on rays that have already been affixed to the floor.

Drag • Erdem Erem and Murat Sağlam

Total time 25 minutes

Aims and outcomes

- To understand that in order to increase speed without increasing thrust, resistance (or drag) has to be reduced.
- To describe ways in which streamlining is achieved and why streamlining is important.

Location

The activities are ideally suited to the school yard or playing field, although a large hall can be used.

Resources required

Three tanks of water, paper towels for hand-drying, five or six pictures and/or photos of different types for boat ranging from speed boats to oil tankers, A4 paper, some colour pencils and some stopwatches.

Misconceptions

The students may incorrectly think that air or water resistance has a fixed value for a particular object irrespective of size or speed.

Process

Warm-up (15 minutes)

All but four of the students arrange themselves in rows across a clear space. They are obstacles that are rooted to the spot with their arms by their sides. The remaining four students *must* arrange themselves into any shape they wish by holding hands (or a piece of paper if hand-holding is inappropriate) and remain in that shape. They need to find the best shape and direction to move through the obstacles in order to reduce the number of impacts with the obstacles. After one group has had a go the students can be rotated around as often as time permits.

The students are now asked, in turn, to place one of their hands in one of the tanks of water and move the palm of their hands parallel with, and then perpendicular to, the direction of motion of their hand, so as to compare the level of difficulty associated with moving their hands in both situations. The students can be asked to compare the movement of their hand through the water with times when they have held their hands out of the window of a moving car.

Streamlined students pass easily through the water.

Activity (10 minutes)

Instructions

The class counts from one to five until each student has a number. The students with the same number form a group. The teacher gives each group a different picture or photo of a boat and asks them to think how they could redesign it, drawing on their experiences earlier in the lesson, to go faster *without* changing the engine in any way. The students present their ideas and the reasons behind them to the rest of the class.

Differentiation

As an experiment the students may be asked to make and fly kites to demonstrate air resistance.

> **Watch out for:** Students need to be careful when passing through the 'obstacles' and avoid getting water from the tanks near electrical sockets. For kite flying safety, please visit http://www.safekids.co.uk/KiteSafety.html.

Electric circuits • Erdem Erem and Murat Sağlam

Total time 25 minutes

Aims and outcomes
- To understand that a circuit needs to be complete in order for a bulb to light.
- To work collaboratively with other students.

Location
The classroom.

Resources required
Connecting wires, a battery, bulb and switch. You will also need one cardboard necklace with an image of an unlit bulb on one side and a lit bulb on the other, one cardboard necklace with an image of a battery, one cardboard necklace with an image of a switch. You will need to print 15 'battery' role cards on which it states: 'The bulb, who is a friend of yours, is annoyed with the switch because it wants to light up but has not received any electricity. However, the switch does not know that the bulb cannot get electricity when it is open.' You will also need to print 15 'switch' role cards on which it states: 'You are open, but the bulb is unlit and this annoys you because you think that the bulb is just being lazy, so you pay the battery a visit to ask their advice.'

Misconceptions
Some students may think that connecting one of the terminals of a battery to a bulb is enough to light the bulb, while others may try to connect the terminals of the battery to the same point on the bulb. There can also be students who believe that electric currents from the terminals clash in the bulb to light it.

Process
Warm-up (10 minutes)

Circuit circle
The teacher and students arrange themselves in a circle. One student is given a cardboard necklace with a symbol of an unlit bulb on one side and a lit bulb on the other side, while a second student is given a cardboard necklace on which there is a symbol for a battery. The teacher takes on the role of a switch and wears a cardboard necklace with a symbol of an open switch on one side and a closed switch on the other. When the teacher turns the closed switch side of the necklace towards the centre of the circle the students hold each other's hands (or a twisted piece of paper if hand-holding is considered inappropriate) and at the same time the student with the battery necklace raises and lowers their necklace and the student with the bulb necklace turns it lit-side out towards the centre of the circle. The teacher flips their necklace to the open switch side, the students stop holding hands, the battery keeps still and the student with the bulb necklace flips it to show the unlit bulb. Different students can assume the roles using the same necklaces.

The teacher then sets up a demonstration circuit consisting of a battery, a bulb, a switch and some connecting wires, and asks the students to predict what would happen to the bulb when they open and close the circuit and whether the position of the bulb, switch and battery makes any difference.

Note: Drawing the circuit diagram on the white board can also help develop a link between the real circuit, the role play and the circuit diagram.

Activity (15 minutes)

Instructions
The teacher now asks the students to arrange themselves in pairs. In each pair one student takes on the role of a battery, while the other will be a switch. The teacher distributes role cards to the students. The improvisation starts with the switch saying to the battery: 'I'm trying to see but even

though I'm open the bulb is not giving out any light – can you tell me why?' The students are all asked to improvise a conversation in which the battery explains why the switch needs to be closed rather than open. After a few minutes a number of pairs present their improvised dialogue to the rest of the class which can be used to start a discussion.

Differentiation

Students with higher academic attainment in the subject can be presented with more complex circuits in which there are multiple bulbs and switches. Students can be asked to consider the switch settings that would be needed for any one or more of the bulbs to light up.

Watch out for: Take care using necklaces due to the potential choking hazard.

Sound – its transmission through solids, liquids and gases ●
Erdem Erem and Murat Sağlam

Total time 20 minutes

Aims and outcomes

- To understand why, in terms of the particle model, sound needs a medium to travel through.
- To recognize that sound travels at different speeds in different types of material.

Location

A large place like a school yard or playing field.

Resources required

A stopwatch, a ball on which is written the word 'Bang' and a pair of cymbals (these can usually be borrowed from a music department).

Process

Warm-up (5 minutes)

Hand circle (see page 127).

Activity (15 minutes)

Instructions

The students arrange themselves into a circle. In the first instance the students are quite close to each other – ideally they can touch each other's finger tips if their arms are fully extended. One student, the starting student, is given a ball with the word 'Bang' written on it. On the left hand side of the starting student is a student with a pair of cymbals. When the teacher asks the starting student to begin they pass the ball to the student on their right. The students must not throw the ball but, instead, they need to place it carefully into the hands of the next student, who in turn passes it to the student to their right, and so on until it reaches the student immediately *before* the student holding the cymbals. Instead of putting the ball into their hands, it is placed by their feet and when so placed the last student strikes the cymbals together to mark the arrival of the 'Bang'.

The teacher (or another student who might not want, or be able, to participate) records the time taken for the ball to make a complete circuit (travelling once around all the students). The students then form themselves into a bigger circle so that the distance between them is at least twice the distance it was in the first circle. They repeat the same process and, again the time taken for the ball to make a complete circuit is recorded. On the third go they form an even bigger circle, with the gap being five or six times the original value, and again record the time taken for the ball to complete a circuit.

The teacher can then use these different times to start a discussion about why it took the ball longer to pass around the circuit when the gaps were larger and whether it would be possible to pass the ball around a circuit if there was a large gap into which students could not go. Developing the analogy to the particulate nature of matter, the teacher can also guide the students towards thinking about the similarities between the spacing in the circle and those within solid, liquids and gases. From here the teacher can encourage the students to make predictions about the speed of sound in various materials.

Note: It is sometimes useful to draw on students' experiences of hearing the whine of an approaching train through the railway lines before they hear its noise through the air.

If the class size is large and space is limited the circle can be turned into a more convoluted shape as long as each student knows who they have to pass the ball to and the distance is set appropriately.

The teacher can use this activity to ask students to predict whether they would expect to hear the sound of bell ringing in a vacuum – a place where the gap between particles is extremely large – and use this to lead into the famous 'bell in a bell-jar' experiment.

Misconceptions

The activity may cause some students to incorrectly believe that sound is an 'entity' or 'substance' while others may arrive to the lesson incorrectly believing that sound moves faster through gasses than through liquids or solids because there is less matter to slow them down.

Differentiation

If you feel it appropriate you might want to use computer simulations to illustrate the propagation of sound waves in the air. A useful and free sound simulation can be downloaded from http://phet. colorado.edu/en/simulation/sound. The simulation may help students realize that sound is a wave carrying energy and needs a medium to move through.

Watch out for: General silliness.

Magnetic fields • Rachael Sharpe

Total time 37 minutes

Aims and outcomes

- To understand that a plotting compass points away from the North Pole end of a bar magnet and towards the South Pole end.
- To recognize that a field line always emerges from a North Pole and enters at a South Pole, that these field lines never cross and are continuous.

Location

Anywhere with a clear floor space on which chalked lines can be drawn (and wiped off).

Resources required

Two flat cardboard cut-out models of the red-end/ blue-end bar magnets (ideally about 4m long and 2.5m wide) with one pole clearly labelled with a large N and the other with a large S, cardboard arrows about 30cm long (it may be an option for the students to make these two bar magnets and the arrows themselves prior to the lesson), some coloured chalk, a digital camera and a damp mop!

Misconceptions

Some students may believe that plotting compasses point to the North Pole and/or that magnetic field lines start and stop at the ends of the magnet rather than being continuous.

Process

Warm-up (7 minutes)

Touch three things (see page 130). These three things could be: a magnetic item, a non-magnetic item and an item that they are uncertain is magnetic or not.

Activity (30 minutes)

Instructions

A single red-end (North Pole)/blue-end (South Pole) bar magnet is placed in the middle of a large clear floor space. The teacher, using the chalk, draws three field lines on the floor either side of the bar magnet *and continues these over the surface of the bar magnet to show that they are continuous*. The role play begins with the students standing and facing away from the North Pole on the drawn field lines. They spread themselves out so that there is enough room and, when asked to, they begin to walk along the field lines entering the South Pole end of the bar magnet and exiting from the North Pole end. After a minute during which the students follow the field lines (the aim being to emphasize their continuous nature) the teacher calls out 'Freeze'. The students, in the role of plotting compasses, now lie down on their backs on the field line (head to toe) where they stand with their heads pointing in the direction they were walking. They position their cardboard plotting compass needle on their stomach with the arrow pointing towards their head. (Ideally at this point the teacher should take an aerial photo of the students for later display/discussion.)

Students acting as plotting compasses placed on the magnetic field lines of a bar magnet.

Then the teacher, having removed the old chalk lines from the floor with the damp mop, now introduces the second bar magnet and positions it so that the two North Poles of the two bar magnets face each other. Students are then asked to position themselves facing the way they think the field lines would move from one of the two magnets. After discussion, the correct field lines are drawn with chalk on the floor and the students walk along these from the North to the South Pole of either magnet. The teacher says 'Freeze', upon which students (in the role of plotting compasses) lie down on their backs on the field line (head to toe) where they stand with their heads pointing in the direction they were walking and their cardboard plotting compass needle on their stomach with the arrow pointing towards their head. Another aerial photo can be taken for display/discussion at this point.

Finally, having removed the old chalk lines as before, the teacher now moves the second bar magnet so that the North Pole of one magnet faces the South Pole of another. The students then work as before to decide and draw (with chalk) the direction of the field lines. The students walk in the direction and then, when the teacher says 'Freeze', the students lie down as before with their cardboard plotting compass needle on their stomach (arrow facing towards their head). Another photo can be taken for display/discussion purposes.

Differentiation

Some students may be able to associate the strength of the magnetic field according to the number of field lines drawn (or, in this activity, the number of students used for the role play). Some students might be able to explore the patterns associated with electromagnetic devices by adapting the same role play.

Watch out for: Students being generally silly with cardboard pieces (such as sharp edges). The teacher needs to ensure students acknowledge their own special awareness and their surroundings to avoid failing over or hitting each other during the activity. There might be issues associated with the taking of photos (climbing a step ladder or on to a table) and the teacher needs to seek advice about this prior to the activity.

The solar system • Rachael Sharpe

Total time 20 minutes

Aims and outcomes

- To recognize that most of our solar system is just empty space.
- To be able to understand the enormous size of our solar system.
- To recognize that display posters showing information about the planets in science departments and/or classrooms do not use the same scale for both the size of the planet and the distances between the planets.

Location

A large, open, space such as a school field or local park.

Resources required

16 teaspoons, two fine grains of salt, four grains of brown crystallized sugar, two grains of white granulated sugar, two kernels of popping corn, two red lentils, four grains of either couscous or millet, glue and/or sellotape to affix one of each of the above onto the bowl of a teaspoon. And a solar garden lamp with a spike on the top of which, centrally, is glued a hazelnut in its shell. You will also need one red and one blue length of plastic tape of each of the following lengths: 1.5m, 2.8m, 3.8m, 5.8m, 19.9m, 36.6m, 73.6m and 115.3m and a tape measure of at least 10m. A flip chart on which is stuck a picture of a rocket (ideally *Voyager 1*) marked in large letters 'Not to scale'. Under this is written 'The fastest man-made object has a speed in this model solar system of 1.6 mm/hour'. The names of the eight planets need to be written on cardboard, twice for each planet, and attached to string to create 16 'planetary' necklaces for students to wear to indicate their role as one of the planets.

Misconceptions

Some students may believe that the planets occupy a large proportion of the solar system and that, relative to their sizes, the distances between them are small. Likewise, many students have a misconception about the size of the solar system, believing that it is much smaller than it actually is.

Process

Warm-up (5 minutes)

Fruit salad (see page 126). Using the names of the planets.

Activity (15 minutes)

Instructions

Arrange 16 students into pairs. To each pair give two planetary necklaces bearing the same planet name. Each pair of students is given two teaspoons into the bowl of which has been stuck the items listed in the resource section. Mercury is represented as a fine grain of salt; Venus and Earth are both grains of crystallized brown sugar; Mars – a grain of granulated sugar; Jupiter – kernel of popping corn; Saturn – a red lentil and Uranus and Neptune are both single grains of couscous or millet.

Move into the middle of the available area and push the solar light firmly into the ground. Give each pair of students a piece of blue and a piece of red plastic of the same length and ask them to attach one end of each around the base of the solar lamp. While the eight students with the red tape, wearing their planetary necklaces, walk away from the metal solar lamp until their tape is taut, those with the blue tape practise pacing out the following distances using the unrolled tape measure: Mercury 10m; Venus 7m; Earth 6m; Mars 5m; Jupiter; 3m; Saturn 2.m; Uranus 1m and Neptune 1m. The remainder of students can stand near the solar lamp to experience the smallness of the eight planets, held out on their teaspoons, relative to the distance between them. The students with the blue tape, also now wearing their planetary necklaces, move away from the metal solar lamp until their string is taut, to join their pair.

To give an idea of the velocity that the planets move at, the teacher asks the students with the blue tape to move clockwise away from their pair, keeping their blue tape taut, as they pace out their practised distance. The distance they move corresponds to the distance moved by their planet in three months.

Note: Mercury's pair of students will appear close together but this is because in three months Mercury will have completed about one complete orbit. Students can be rotated to allow all to have a go and/or students could be allocated roles within the asteroid belt between Mars and Jupiter. Asteroids are of varying sizes but a single grain of flour stuck to a piece of sellotape provides a rough idea of the fact that they are much smaller than Mercury.

Differentiation

Academically more able students might try to calculate the speed of light in this scaled down solar system or calculate the scale speed of a jumbo jet and the time it would take to travel between any two chosen planets.

> **Watch out for:** Students being generally silly with the tapes and warn about the risk of tripping.

7 Physics: session plans for 14–16

This chapter contains the following session plans

Braking distance • Ian Abrahams

Total time 30 minutes

Aims and outcomes

- To make and test predictions about the factors affecting stopping distance.
- To measure and record distances.
- To identify patterns in data and be able to make predictions based on these.

Location

Ideally this is best undertaken out of doors.

Resources required

One or two long tape measures to mark off 50–100m, stopwatch (or students' own watches), a bag of coloured counters, some plastic tape, large self-adhesive badges labelled 'kinetic energy', 'brakes', 'timekeeper' and 'driver', two bags: one labelled 'kinetic energy', the other 'heat energy'.

Misconceptions

Many students do not grasp that for an object to stop it needs to transform all of its kinetic energy into heat using brakes. Many are also unaware that brakes are only able to transfer so much kinetic energy into heat energy every second which is why it takes a moving object, such as a car, time to stop.

Process

Warm-up (5 minutes)

Hand circle (see page 127).

Activity (25 minutes)

Outline

In this activity students mime being in a car and, in order to stop the car, are required to transform its total kinetic energy, in the form of 'energy' counters, via the car's brakes, which are able do so only at a fixed rate. By varying the speed of the car, and hence its kinetic energy, the time required for the brakes to convert all of the car's kinetic energy into heat can be measured. By doubling, tripling, quadrupling the car's initial speed the time taken to transform the kinetic energy to heat will be found to increase as the square of the increase made i.e. 4, 9, 16 times the initial time respectively.

Instructions

1. Allocate roles: per group of four students you will want one student as the driver who carries a board with their speed clearly displayed, one student carries the car's kinetic energy in a bag marked 'kinetic energy', one student is the brakes and carries an empty bag marked 'heat energy', another student is the timekeeper. The four students can be tied together using tape to make a 'car unit'. I like having a starter to wave a flag to set the cars off together and an official recorder who measures the braking distance of each group using the tape measures.
2. Lay the tape along a stretch of open ground.
3. The tricky bit is that you need to calculate the energy efficiency of the brakes that will convert all of a car's kinetic energy, at its maximum speed, into heat by the time the students have walked to the end of the tape, assuming that they can transfer one kinetic energy counter to the brakes about every 4 seconds. You can also adjust the mass of the car to help you meet this aim.
4. The role of the timekeeper is to call out 'Now' every four seconds so that the student marked 'kinetic energy' knows to pass a single counter to the brakes who puts it into their 'heat' bag.
5. Line the groups of four students up level with the end of the tape with the cars arranged with increasing speed.
6. The instructions to the students are that the groups *all* walk at the *same* speed. A group stops as soon as the last counter of kinetic energy has been transferred into the brakes' 'heat' bag.

7. With a few runs through you can obtain a really nice staggered finishing line with the distance increasing as the square of the speed indicated on the drivers' boards.

Note: during the activity students should be encouraged to use the words/terms 'kinetic energy', 'heat energy', 'transformed' and 'conservation of energy'. The meaning of these should be made clear when opportunities present themselves and be reinforced throughout the activity.

Differentiation

More able students can calculate their car's own kinetic energy and investigate the effect of keeping speed the same and varying mass. Students often note that there is a time lag between the timekeeper saying 'Now' and the brakes passing over the kinetic energy counter and this is a good opportunity to link in with 'thinking distance' and reflex times.

> **Watch out for:** The main issue here is that students can get excited about the idea of being tied together with tape, so please use your professional judgement as to whether to remove and/or adapt this part of the task as you see fit.

P-waves and S-waves • Ian Abrahams

Total time 15 minutes

Aims and outcomes

- To make and test predictions about the transfer of kinetic energy in earthquakes through P-waves and S-waves.
- To identify and make predictions from patterns in data.

Location

Ideally in a room with sufficient space for 27 students to stand, arms outstretched on each other's shoulders in a 3 × 9 arrangement with a few metres clear around them.

Resources required

Three stacks of wooden/plastic blocks to represent buildings – each stack to be at least 0.5m high. A flip chart on which is written 'Not to scale'.

Misconceptions

This activity can generate/reinforce a misconception about the relative size of atoms and the spaces between them.

Process

Warm-up (5 minutes)

Fruit salad (see page 126). Use terms such as 'P-wave', 'S-wave', 'transverse', 'longitudinal', 'mantle', 'liquids', 'solids' and 'core'.

Activity (10 minutes)

Outline

This activity provides students with a visual model of P-waves and S-waves. Constructing this model enables students to experience why P-waves, but not S-waves, can travel through liquids.

Instructions

1. Allocate roles: 27 students form a 3 × 9 arrangement (this can be made longer or shorter depending on the number of students). Ask another three students to be starters. They ideally wear lab coats or some other garment to distinguish them from the other students and they stand behind the back row of three students and are responsible for starting the wave. In each of the three columns each student places their hands, arms outstretched, on the shoulders of the person in front of them.

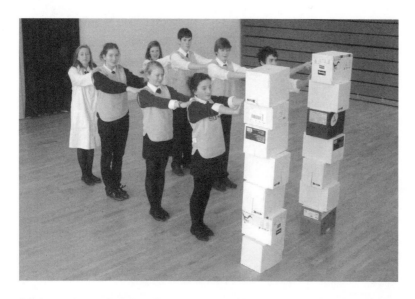

Students places their hands, arms outstretched, on the shoulders of the person in front of them.

2. For a P-wave (longitudinal) in a solid the three starters simultaneously push gently forward on the three students in the back row. The resulting forward motion, which each row successively passes on to the shoulders of the row in front of it, will travel along the line.

3. The three students in the final front row push the stack of blocks over *forwards*.

4. For a S-wave (transverse) in a solid the starters simultaneously gently push each of the three students in the back row sideways by pushing sideways on each of those three students' left (or right) shoulder and then pull them back into line again before repeating the process but this time pushing on the opposite shoulder.

5. The three students in the final front row knock the stack of blocks over sideways.

6. For a P-wave (longitudinal) in a liquid ask each of the nine rows to move apart so that with their hands outstretched they are a few centimetres away from touching the shoulders of the person in the row in front of them. The three starters again simultaneously push gently forward on the three students in the back row. While the first three students are not initially touching the shoulders of those in front of them, the initial push from the starters closes that gap and the resulting forward motion, which each row successively passes on to the shoulders of the row in front of it, will again be seen to travel along the line (albeit slightly slower as the students have to cover more space in order to transmit their forward motion).

7. The three students in the final front row push the stack of blocks over *forwards*.

8. For a S-wave (transverse) in a liquid ask each of the nine rows to again move apart so that with their hands outstretched they are a few centimetres away from touching the shoulders of the person in the row in front of them. The starters again simultaneously gently push each of the three students in the back row sideways by pushing sideways (they should be careful not to impart any forward motion) on each of those three students' left (or right) shoulder and then pull them back into line again before repeating the process but, this time, pushing on the opposite shoulder. As the hands of the three students in the back row are not touching the shoulders of the students in front of them, and no forward motion has been imparted to them by the starters, this solely sideways motion cannot be transferred down each of the three columns.

9. The stack of blocks remains standing.

10. A large poster, on which is written 'Not to scale', is displayed prominently throughout this activity.

Note: During the activity students should be encouraged to use the words/terms 'P-waves', 'longitudinal waves', 'S-waves' and 'transverse waves' and the meaning of these should be made clear when opportunities present themselves and be reinforced throughout the activity.

Differentiation

This task can be developed further by marking on the floor a cross-section of the Earth and arranging the students so that those standing on 'solid' material have their hands on the shoulders of the student in the row in front of them while at a solid/liquid boundary the gap increases by those few centimetres. Here the P-waves and S-waves both pass through the solid but the solid/liquid boundary only permits the passage of P-waves and the destruction of the stack of blocks in front of the P-wave students.

Watch out for: The main issue here is that students can get excited about the idea of shaking each other and/or pushing each other over and so guidance about not being silly is advised.

Static electricity • Ian Abrahams

Total time 20 minutes

Aims and outcomes

- To understand how and why a statically charged object can be attracted to an uncharged object.

Location

The classroom or a teaching room with a clear floor space.

Resources required

Ten balloons (attached to strings so they can be fastened to students). On four of these are drawn, using an appropriate marker pen, lots of '-ve' and '+ve' symbols in the ratio 3:1 respectively (to clearly show a -ve charge imbalance). On the remaining six balloons a large single '-ve' symbol is drawn (you might choose to write '1 electron'). A minimum of four 'negatively charged balloon' headbands, or other means of identifying those students taking on the role of the statically charged balloon. Six headbands, or an alternative, to identify a minimum of six students as positively charged atomic nuclei and a further six headbands, or other means of identification, for those six students taking on the roles of single electrons. A flip chart on which is written 'Not to scale'. A large cardboard cut out of a hand or an arrow on which is written 'Push' and a marker pen suitable for drawing on balloons.

Misconceptions

Some students may think that objects that have a net zero charge cannot have a localized charge imbalance. This role play can reinforce misconceptions about the relative size of electrons and the atomic nucleus.

Process

Warm-up (5 minutes)

Keepy uppy (see page 128).

Activity (15 minutes)

The teacher draws a long rectangle 4m × 0.5m on the floor to represent a wall within which they draw six, equally spaced, small circles each about 0.5m apart. Each of the six students taking the role of the positively charged atomic nuclei stands in a circle and is told that they are fixed to that spot. Around each of one of those six students another student, representing a single outer shell electron, slowly revolves (taking care not to collide into the other revolving electrons) each with a balloon attached to them on which is drawn a *single* large '-ve'. The teacher informs the class that, as with like and unalike poles of a magnet, like charges repel each other while unlike attract.

The role play starts off with the single negatively charged electron revolving around the nucleus. The four students representing the negatively charged balloon hold hands (if holding hands is not appropriate then make short strips of paper for students to hold together) and a student holding the 'hand' cut out or the 'Push' arrow pushes them towards the six positively charged atomic nuclei. As they approach the single negatively charged electrons that are revolving around the six positively charged atomic nuclei, the four students representing the negatively charged balloon begin to grimace to show their dislike (repulsion) at being pushed towards other negative charges. As they get nearer, the six electrons revolving around the six positively charged atomic nuclei cease to revolve and move to the far side of the six positively charged atomic nuclei (I like them to also turn their backs to reinforce the repulsion) to keep away from the approaching four students. Until the six electrons have moved to the far side and turned their backs, the pushing 'hand' or 'Push' arrow needs to make out that it's really hard work (they are effectively having to overcome the initial electrostatic repulsion). As soon as the six electrons have turned their backs, the four approaching students are able to link hands (or paper strips) with four of the six positively charged atomic nuclei, illustrating that the balloon has now become 'attached' to the wall through a localized charge imbalance.

Note: You might like to use freeze frame at critical points in the role play to focus the discussion on what is happening at that specific point.

Display the 'Not to scale' flip chart prominently next to the role play and make it clear to the students that this role play does not reflect the actual relative sizes of electrons or nuclei.

Differentiation

For high-ability groups you might allocate roles but allow the students the opportunity to try to work out a mechanism to explain how a statically charged balloon is attracted to a wall that has a net neutral electric charge. Lower academic attainment groups might need slightly more guidance but in general this role play is suitable for all students in the form outlined above.

> **Watch out for:** Silly behaviour that can lead to student–student collisions.

Radioactivity – half-life • Ian Abrahams and Rachael Sharpe

Total time 25 minutes

Aims and outcomes

- To understand the nature of half-life.
- To understand the characteristic feature of half-life decay.

Location

Ideally this is best undertaken out of doors or in a hall with clear floor space.

Resources required

A stopwatch, two green 10m long strips of coloured tape, one 15m strip of red tape and a similar length of yellow tape. Two large pieces of cardboard – on one is written 'Number of decayed particles, on the other 'Time'. Sticky tape, or 10–14 tent pegs to fix the various tapes to the ground or floor. You will also need ten A4 pieces of cardboard, on each of which is written '1 minute', a 15m length of rope or thick wool and a dice for each student and one for the teacher.

Misconceptions

Some students believe that in every half-life period the same number of atoms decays rather than half of the total number of radioactive atoms that have yet to decay. Likewise, some students think half-life decay always results in exactly half the expected number of atoms decaying rather than recognizing the probabilistic nature of such decay. This role play can sometimes introduce a belief that there is a 'hidden variable' that determines whether or not a particular atom decays at a particular time.

Process

Warm-up (5 minutes)

Fruit salad (see page 126). Use terms such as 'radioactivity', 'half-life', 'exponential', 'decay', 'probabilistic' and 'random'.

Activity (20 minutes)

Outline

There are essentially two parts to this activity. In the first students, in the role of radioactive atoms, toss a dice to randomly determine whether or not they decay within a given fixed time span. The second part of the activity uses axes, affixed to the ground/floor, to make up a human bar chart on which a student, once their atom has decayed, stands in the appropriate place. Once all atoms have decayed the rope is held by the top person in each student column to show the exponential shape of the decay.

Note: Using two or more classes studying this topic (or repeating the process more than once with the same class to produce average results) generates results that, when plotted, better reflect an exponential decay.

Instructions

1. Allocate roles: all students are radioactive atoms.
2. Lay the two lengths of tape along the ground/floor as X and Y axes and fix them into place using sticky tape or tent pegs.
3. Fix the cardboard axis labels in place in a similar manner.
4. Along the X axis place at every metre one of the '1 minute' A4 cards.
5. Fix these cards in place in a similar fashion.
6. Give each student a dice and tell them to toss (and catch!) it when you tell them to.
7. Within the space of *1 minute* the teacher needs to ask the students to (a) toss and catch their dice (b) separate into six clear groups based on the result of their dice toss (make sure they are clearly separated so that they cannot swap groups once they learn which group has

decayed!). The teacher then tosses their own dice *twice* (this makes the process quicker). Whatever two results the teacher gets (if the same outcome is obtained on the second throw toss again until a different result is obtained) those students with either of those two same results have 'decayed'. (c) The first group of decayed students move to make the first student column on the bar chart above the first '1 minute' piece of cardboard on the X axis. The task is then repeated every 1 minute until the last student has decayed and moved over, and onto, the bar chart.

Note: It takes a bit of practice to complete each cycle of the activity every minute but the students soon get used to it and without this the task can drag on too long.

8. The rope is then passed to the top person in each column, and placed under their foot on the ground/floor, to produce a line rope graph that shows exponential decay.

9. Ascertain the point on the Y axis that corresponds to half the number of students in the class – pin the red tape to this point on the Y axis and then project it across, parallel to the X axis, until it intersects with the rope and then, after asking a student to hold it in place, project it directly down to the X axis and pin it in place. Total up the time from the origin to that point approximating the value in the final '1 minute' column if not exact.

10. This is the students' half-life 'period'.

11. Go along the X axis for another half-life period and pin the end of the yellow tape to the X axis at this point.

12. Project the yellow tape directly up to the point at which it intersects the rope. Then, after asking a student to hold it in place, project it directly across, parallel to the X axis, until it meets the Y axis and pin it in place.

13. The point on the Y axis should be approximately equal to half of the number of students who first decayed or about a quarter of the students in the class.

Differentiation

More able students can consider the reason the results are not ideal and consider what they might have to do to achieve a more ideal set of results. By recognizing that a more ideal result can be achieved by using much larger numbers of students a realization can be achieved that the predictive success of half-life techniques is based on the truly astronomically large number of radioactive atoms in a sample.

> **Watch out for:** Take care with so many tapes and ropes on the floor as these can present a tripping hazard.

Force and acceleration • Murat Sağlam and Erdem Erem

Total time 20 minutes

Aims and outcomes

- To understand that a force acting on an object will cause a change in its state of rest or motion.
- To recognize that an object's acceleration depends on *both* the force *and* the mass.
- That force, mass and acceleration are related by the equation: Force = mass × acceleration.

Location

Classroom and/or school yard.

Resources required

A4 paper, one tennis ball, one soccer ball, one leather or rubber medicine ball with a mass of 5kg or more.

Misconceptions

Some students may believe that speed, velocity and acceleration are the same and/or that a constant force cannot produce an acceleration because it is not, itself, getting any larger.

Process

Warm-up (10 minutes)

Ask the students to form themselves into groups of about ten – the important point is that the groups have an even number of students. If there is a student left over you can allocate them the role of referee. Each group then forms two parallel lines 5m apart, with an equal number of students in each line. Starting with the lightest ball, the students at the starting end of each line roll the ball along the corridor between the two rows. When the student at the finish end of the line has received the ball, they run with the ball back to the starting end and the student who rolled it runs up to the finishing end of the line. The process is repeated until the students have returned to their initial starting position. The same process is repeated next with the ball with the intermediate mass and finally with the ball with the largest mass. On completion the teacher discusses with the students (a) which ball was easier to roll and why, (b) which ball required more force to roll to the other side and (c) which ball was easier to accelerate.

Note: The balls must *not* be thrown, only rolled.

Activity (10 minutes)

Instructions

The students arrange themselves into pairs in which one assumes the role of a car dealer while the other takes on the role of a customer wanting to buy a lorry. The teacher puts the following instructions on the board as a way of starting the 'free-style' role play off:

Scenario: Customer and car salesman are on a test drive

Car salesman (who understands physics and F=ma): 'This 10-ton lorry has a big and very powerful engine.'

Customer (who has no understanding of physics): 'But this lorry takes ages to speed up, even my small ½-ton car has better acceleration.'

The teacher asks the students to improvise how the discussion might develop and, as they move from pair to pair, they draw the students' attention to the ideas of mass, force and how the formula F = ma can help explain why the little car with a small engine might still have a faster acceleration than the big, heavy lorry with a bigger, more powerful, engine.

Differentiation

If the students are able to handle numerical calculations specific values for force, mass and acceleration can be introduced into the animation.

> **Watch out for:** Take care when using the medicine ball.

Energy • Murat Sağlam and Rachael Sharpe

Total time 25 minutes

Aims and outcomes

- To be able to describe complex energy transformations using Sankey diagrams.

Location

The classroom.

Resources required

Laminated pictures (A4 size) of a range of items that transform energy from one form to another – e.g. a hydro-electric dam, wind turbine, toaster, car, tree, aeroplane – that have been made into necklaces or crown-like hats. A selection of A4 laminated sheets, made into necklaces, labelled with the various forms of energy e.g. 'chemical', 'kinetic', 'gravitational potential', 'heat' and 'light'. A selection of cardboard arrows of various shapes and sizes – again, these can either be made into necklaces or simply be available to be hand-held or a mixture of both.

Misconceptions

Instead of understanding energy as a conserved quality, some students may believe that it is created, destroyed and/or used up.

Process

Warm-up (5 minutes)

Keepy uppy (see page 128).

Activity (20 minutes)

Instructions

The laminated pictures and forms of energy as well as a selection of arrows are placed in different locations around the classroom and the students, in groups of five (or more if appropriate), are allocated to one picture. Students are given 2 minutes to represent the energy transformations by wearing the laminated cards and arrows so as to form a human Sankey diagram. Each group then presents their human Sankey diagram to the rest of the class and changes in the form of the Sankey diagram can be made in terms of further additions and/or subtractions.

The class is now split into two groups and, after all of the laminated energy cards have been mixed up, they are divided randomly between the two groups so that each group has the same number of cards. Each group has to design a process which involves complex energy transformations and that uses all of their cards. In each part of the process in which an energy transformation occurs a student, or group of students, have to mime that part of the process. It is a requirement that every student within the group has a role in the animation. After 10 minutes the groups present their animations to the other group in such a way that it is seen to unfold chronologically from the start of the process to its end and, as each stage in the process is completed, the students in that stage freeze. The other groups need to try to ascertain what the process was and comment on the appropriateness of the energy transformations that were depicted.

Students form a human Sankey diagram.

Differentiation

It might be desirable, with some groups of students, to allocate the process for the animation so as to ensure an appropriate level of complexity according to the needs and abilities of the students.

Watch out for: Students need to take care when hanging items around their necks.

Alpha, beta and gamma absorption • Rachael Sharpe

Total time 25 minutes

Aims and outcomes

- To understand the nature of alpha, beta and gamma radiation.
- To understand the penetrating power of alpha, beta and gamma radiation.

Location

The classroom or a teaching room with a clear floor space.

Resources required

A roll of lining paper (cheap and easy to get hold of from DIY stores and decorators' merchants), a few rolls of aluminium foil, a sheet of plywood approximately 2m × 2m, painted grey and covered with the symbol 'Pb' and the word 'lead', a plywood sinusoidal wave about 2m long. Four wooden broom handles. One large, plain white t-shirt which is covered with the words 'electron' and 'beta particle' and the symbols 'β' and '-e', two large, plain red t-shirts covered with the words 'proton' and '+ ve', two large, plain green t-shirts covered with the words 'neutron' and 'no charge'. You will also need a plain white bed sheet. Cut a length-wise strip of the sheet approximately 10cm wide and cover this with the words 'helium nucleus' and 'α'. Along the middle of the remainder of the sheet cut five holes each large enough for a head to pass through and cover the sheet with the words 'gamma ray' and the symbol 'γ'.

Note: D&T departments are often able to construct or offer advice about how to construct the plywood sinusoidal wave. The t-shirts can be purchased relatively cheaply from charity shops and, once washed, can be used every year.

Misconceptions

Some students confuse alpha and beta radiation with electromagnetic radiation – a misconception made worse by the fact that gamma radiation is an electromagnetic radiation. This role play can generate the misconception that the alpha and beta particles and gamma rays do not enter into the material of the barriers whereas, in fact, they do.

Process

Warm-up (5 minutes)

Fruit salad (see page 126). Use terms such as 'alpha particle', 'beta particle', 'gamma ray', 'helium nucleus', 'electron', 'electro-magnetic radiation', 'penetrating' and 'absorption'.

Activity (20 minutes)

Outline

This role play has a 'wow' factor that helps anchor students' understanding of the physics with the aid of a memorable visual experience.

Instructions

1. Allocate roles so that four students are together as an alpha particle, one student is alone as a beta particle and five students are together as the gamma ray.
2. The beta particle wears the 'beta particle' t-shirt over their school shirt.
3. Two of the four alpha particle students wear the 'proton' t-shirt over their school shirts while the other two wear the 'neutron' t-shirt over their school shirts. Once in their t-shirts, they form themselves into a unit with their backs to each other and they are tied together around their waists with the strip of the sheet covered with the words 'helium nucleus' and 'α'.
4. The five gamma ray students place the sheet over them with their heads protruding through the five holes and hold the plywood sinusoidal wave with their right (or left) hands.

5. Two students, one on each side, hold two strips of lining paper between them wound around a broom handle, a bit like a scroll, so as to make a taut paper 'barrier'. (Note: the lining paper needs to be scored with a sharp knife so that when a student runs into it gives way easily.)

6. Behind them two further students, one on each side, hold two strips of aluminium foil between them that have been wound around a broom handle (again like a taut scroll) to form an aluminium foil 'barrier'. (Note: The aluminium foil, as with the lining paper, needs to be scored with a sharp knife so that when a student runs into it gives way easily.)

7. Behind them two students, one on either side, support the 'lead' plywood sheet.

8. The alpha particle moves very slowly towards the lining paper barrier as if finding it difficult to pass through the air. On reaching the paper barrier, they pretend to be unable to pass through it and, after a very brief struggle, collapse to the floor.

9. Next the lone beta particle, having punched the air like a prize fighter, runs at the paper barrier and tears straight through it. Yet, when they reach the aluminium barrier, they pretend to be unable to pass through it and, after a few moments of struggle, collapse to the floor.

10. Replace the paper barrier and remember to score the sheets again.

11. The gamma ray does an elaborate sumo wrestler-style foot-stamping performance and then charges at the paper barrier, passing straight through it, then on to, and straight through, the aluminium barrier. They are only stopped by the 'lead' barrier where they put up a considerable struggle, pushing hard at the barrier before, after about 15 seconds, collapsing to the floor.

Students holding up the paper and aluminium barriers with the 'lead' screen seen behind them.

The beta particle about to set off to pass through the paper before being stopped by the aluminium sheet.

The gamma ray about to pass through the paper and aluminium before being stopped by the lead screen.

Watch out for: Warn students not to collide with the plywood and to watch their eyes when it comes to the torn aluminium foil. Ensure care is taken when scoring material with a sharp knife. Ensure students are careful to avoid paper cuts.

8 Conclusions

Martin Braund

Two cultures or one way of learning?

It might seem odd to some scientists and science teachers that in this book we have drawn on an 'arts' subject (drama) to teach the 'sciences'. Unfortunately many reading this book will have grown up in a world where the 'arts' are seen as separate from the 'sciences', each having developed its own distinctive, separate cultural and academic capital – rarely the twain have met. The school system has tended to accentuate this notion of a divide between the arts (with humanities) and science, technology and mathematics by timetabling and management structures, different environments for teaching and the way teachers are trained.

Many of us involved in this book were products of this system, forced to choose at an early age between the arts and the sciences. Thus for the first five of my seven years in my senior school I was placed into an arts stream because I was 'good at' languages, history and English literature. But my real love was biology and it took me months of hard graft to make up the ground in basic chemistry and physics when I finally moved to a science sixth form. It is not just this shoehorning of assumed interest and talent at an early age that is wrong. It is also the assumption that scientists are lone figures pursuing obscure subjects with a cold and logical approach, divorced from the emotions and responsibilities of normal life and work. Unfortunately this is what many school students think scientists are like and it is one of the main reasons why they are put off school science and so few study sciences at a higher level or take it up as a career.

The two cultures (arts and sciences) notion was a product of the eighteenth, nineteenth and early twentieth centuries when the great academies and societies evolved and sought to protect their members' kudos and interests. Earlier, it was not so clear that the arts and sciences should make distinct contributions to human existence. We only have to think back to the days of the renaissance and two of the greatest figures of 'the arts' to expose the fallacy of the two cultures. We may know of Leonardo Da Vinci's abilities with engineering and mechanical propulsion as well as painting but how many know that Michelangelo engineered Florence's military defences and was an expert on human anatomy (you have only to look at the way he showed muscles and veins on his greatest sculptures to realize this)?

In more modern times, the scientist and writer Peter Medawar critiqued the outdated and restricted view of scientists' talents and interests. In *The Limits of Science* he wrote: 'There are poet scientists and philosopher scientists and even a few mystics . . . and most people who are in fact scientists could easily have been something else instead' (p.11). In the 1950s novelist and scientist C. P. Snow delivered a lecture at Cambridge on the dangers of the growing schism between the arts and sciences and the damage this was doing to education (see Snow, 1993). In Snow's view the rivalries and jealousies between the two cultures dominated education development in the mid twentieth century but limited progressive ideas. Today there is some hope that a more progressive, holistic view is emerging among scientists. For example, Nobel astrophysicist George Smoot sees the 'two cultures' as an outmoded idea, irrelevant to the modern world. He claims we are now entering a 'third culture' more heavily dominated by science and technology.

Basically, in terms of whatever war (between the two cultures) has been going on, I think it has finished. I don't characterize it by saying we (the scientists) have won. I think everybody has won. We are living in a profound science culture and the big events that are affecting people's lives are scientific ones.

(George Smoot as quoted in an article by
Tim Adams in the *Observer*, 1 July 2007)

I have always believed the arts can offer much to learning science and it is worth noting justifications used for arts education (including drama) include helping develop general and specific (scientific) cognitive capacity. Justifications have commonly been made from the perspective of neurobiology. Since the mid nineteenth century there was increasing evidence, from studies of patients with brain impairments, that the left and right hemispheres of the cerebral cortex might be differentiated and hence control different physical and cognitive functions. Sperry's Nobel prize-winning research on patients with severed *corpus callosa* (the region between the two hemispheres) showed language ability was clearly associated with left hemisphere function and discrimination of shape and design with the right (Sperry, 1966). Drawing on Sperry's work, Herrmann went on to postulate different abilities and types of thinking associated with the two hemispheres. Analytical and sequential reasoning (and thus science) was said to be associated with the left hemisphere while the right deals with interpersonal, imaginative and emotional thinking (Herrmann, 1990). This led some to a rather unsophisticated, reductionist, view that the arts are about the right side of the brain and science and mathematics the left, a view likely to exacerbate the two cultures divisions. However, many have challenged the location of, what Gardner (1983) later called 'hypothetical-deductive reasoning', in the left side of the brain. An often quoted example is mathematically gifted children who tend to be left-handed and therefore have right hemisphere dominance (the right brain controls left side body movements). Reading about these linkages led drama educator Dorothy Heathcote to advocate drama activity as a way to strengthen scientific reasoning, as the right-hemisphere activity could lead to a 'left-handed way of knowing', that is thus more 'scientific' (Wagner,1979). Modern brain biology has challenged the ideas supporting separate brain functions and, in his very useful review of the field, Morris points out that most cognitive scientists and educators today favour a more 'whole brain function view', acknowledging that activities drawing on a wide a range of stimulation as possible inevitably improve brain function, especially for higher order activity and critical thinking (singsurf.org, 2010). Whatever position you take, the role of the arts and, in particular, of drama cannot be ignored in developing the reasoning needed for good scientific thinking.

How drama can help in the teaching and learning of science

To see how drama helps learning in science it is necessary to develop a simple model. The model has two purposes. First to help draw together two fields of thinking, in science education and drama and, second, to provide a means through which the use of drama activities in science teaching can be better understood and evaluated by teachers. For the purposes of the model, learning science is seen as a process rationalizing two worlds of knowing, the learner's world and the scientist's. The learner's world draws on everyday experience, commonly used terms and language and what has been gleaned from science as presented knowledge from media and from family, friends and school. The scientist's world of knowing, which is the eventual target for learning change, has specific rational explanations for the world based on applications of concepts and theories mediated by empirical validation. This view can be represented as a *general model for learning science*, (see Figure 1). In this general model 'cognitive dissonance' is the 'distance' between the two worlds of knowing and the 'experiential space' is the nature of activity and effort, used by the teacher, to reduce the amount of cognitive dissonance and so close the gap between the two worlds. This is what good science teachers are always trying to do.

Figure 1. A general model for learning science.

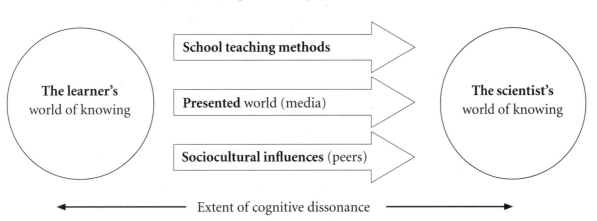

Experiential 'space'

So, now to make this general model specific to using drama (See Figure 2). In this second model, the space between the learner's ways of knowing and the scientist's way of knowing is bridged by the 'drama space'. Though the 'space' is not empty in terms of the learner's existing ideas the methods used by the teacher, their confidence and skill at using them and the learner's efficacy (belief about learning value) and attitudes to drama as a learning method also populate the space and must be taken into account to ensure success of teaching. It could be argued that these models could be used more widely than for drama – perhaps for many approaches in the sociocultural landscape of learning. Hence the word 'drama' could be substituted with 'practical work', 'group task' and so on.

Figure 2. A model for drama as a way of learning science.

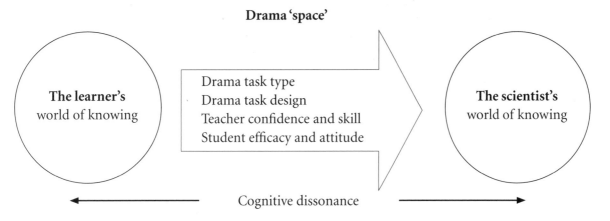

Drama 'space'

However, what makes drama special to consider using this model, and sometimes more demanding for teachers to use than other forms of learning in an 'active' tradition, are the particular pedagogical features and decisions that must be taken to get the most from any particular task and that are unique to different forms of drama task. As Dorion points out, from classroom studies of just one type – physical role plays – these events require complex analogies and continuous combinations of implicit and explicit anthropomorphism (Dorion, 2009). Whatever type of drama is used by teachers there is inevitably going to be a question of the extent of 'pedagogical border crossing' required from the pedagogy (teaching methods) of drama to the pedagogy of science, to make drama useful as a tool for learning. For some teachers the border crossing is not so great, they feel comfortable with drama and methods used by dramatists and drama educators, for others the crossing is difficult or never made and this could be a question of how they see the nature of science and how it is best understood.

In this book we have provided a comprehensive range of activities covering a range of topics often taught in physical and natural sciences to learners aged between 11 and 16. We have thought carefully about two aspects of the model of how we see drama contributing to learning science that occupy the drama space, that is: the type of drama and the design of the task itself. The last of the three areas is the teacher's confidence and skill at using the tasks. This is something that will develop as you use, and become more confident with, these tasks and in this respect your professionalism, and desires to help make abstract ideas more available to students using the tasks in this book, will help that confidence and skill grow.

And, as your confidence in using drama increases and drama becomes a more regular part of your teaching repertoire, the obvious next step will be for you to experiment with new ideas of your own. While we, for example, have chosen to use props in our sessions there is no reason for you not to experiment in using 'prop-free' drama or at least drama sessions that have far fewer props. So, while we have suggested that students identify themselves a various items, for example, using labels, necklaces or hats, you could instead ask them to use their bodies to represent these items. You might suggest, for example, that a student poses with their sleeves rolled up making 'muscles' to represent a battery, or that a student jumping about with their hands waving is a lit bulb while a student hunched up and frozen is an unlit one. In my own experience I found that my students really liked coming up with novel ideas of how to represent different objects or materials in physics lessons and that their own ideas were not only often better than my own but, in coming up with their own ideas, they took a greater sense of ownership of the work. That said, there is certainly a need for students to be allowed to learn to walk before setting them off running and our own experience, as well as that of the teachers we have worked with, is that familiarizing the students with the use of drama using the highly structured and well tested sessions in this book provides them with the basic skills that they will then be able to use in the more 'freestyle' approach that you might be working towards using.

Finally, whether you are using the sessions in this book or ones that you have gone on to develop your guiding question should remain: to what extent is this activity effective in reducing the cognitive dissonance between the idea as it is in the world of 'knowing science' and a learner's understanding of that idea? We wish you well in these endeavours.

Appendix 1: Warm-up exercises

Bidi Iredale

This appendix contains the following warm-up exercises

These six warm-up exercises can be used in conjunction with the subject specific role plays in the book. Each exercise or game has been tried and tested and developed in the classroom or science lab with teachers and their students. As you become more familiar with these there is no reason for you not to experiment and see whether you prefer using a different one from the one we have suggested.

Fruit salad

Can be used to introduce both a topic and/or use new vocabulary as well as mixing up members of a group and encouraging listening and speaking. Players have to change seats in the circle and avoid being left in the middle of the circle without a seat.

Materials

Circle of chairs.

Instructions

Players sit in a circle on chairs. One player without a chair stands in the middle of the circle. The leader names the players, for example, 'apple', 'orange' and 'banana', in order around the circle, ending with the player standing in the middle. Players have to remember their fruit. (It's a good idea to check that all players remember their fruit; perhaps ask all bananas to stand up, all apples to kneel and all oranges to stay seated.) The player in the middle without a seat calls out either 'apple', 'orange' or 'banana'. If the player in the middle calls out 'orange' then all those players who are an orange must leave their seats and find an empty chair to sit in. The player in the middle also takes this opportunity to sit in one of the empty chairs. The player then left in the middle without a seat calls out the name of one of the fruits and the game continues. The player left in the middle may also call out 'fruit salad' and then *all* the players must change their seats.

Tips

- It's a good idea for players to lay claim to an empty chair by putting their hand on it before sitting on it. The game tends to be pretty energetic and chairs can fall backwards if sat on wildly.
- The game can be played without chairs by using small rounds of matting on the floor.
- The players cannot move to the chairs directly next to the one they were just sitting on or return to the seat they have just left.

Additions and variations

- The 'recipe' of the game can be changed to suit the subject of the session, e.g. planets in the solar system, members of the electromagnetic spectrum or organs of the body.
- Instead of calling out the name of an item, like the name of a fruit, the players can perform a previously agreed action or mime which symbolizes that item.
- Players might make double-sided flash cards with the name of the item on, or its picture, and the cards could be held up instead of the names called out.

Hand circle

Can be used to focus the group and bring them all together in one activity at the beginning of the session. The players must pass the slap or pat around the circle of hands, without missing out a hand, as quickly and smoothly as possible

Instructions

All players kneel in a circle placing their hands in front of them palms down, thereby forming a circle of hands. Alternately, players can stand around a large bench or table and place hands palm down on the bench or table. The leader begins by slapping first their right, then their left, palm on the surface (floor or table). The hand next to the leader's hand then slaps the surface, then the next hand in the circle and so on around the circle. The slap or pat can then be sent the other way around the circle.

Once players have achieved the first part then they can move on to the next stage where players place their hands in a circle so as no two hands belonging to the same person are next to each other (the players' hands are placed alternately around the circle). Pass the pat around the circle again so it passes from each adjacent hand to the next. Everyone concentrates on staring at the next hand to move. It can be a strange sensation staring at the next hand, willing it to move, then realizing that it is your hand!

Tips

- Encourage the group to play the game without speaking.
- The leader has the power to control the game by 'collecting' the slaps (i.e. making a grabbing action with their hand or making the action of putting them in their pocket etc) as they come round the circle to them.
- Once the group knows the game other players can take on the role of leader.
- The game can be used as a starter and the players are already in a circle for the following activity when appropriate.

Additions and variations

- If a player quickly slaps their palm down twice then the slap is sent back around the circle in the opposite direction.
- Three slaps in a row means that the next hand is missed out.
- The game can be played standing up and using feet instead of hands.

Keepy uppy

Can be used to encourage group co-operation, concentration, coordination and to generate appropriate vocabulary. Players must work as a group to keep a ball up in the air.

Materials

Small softball and a clear space

Instructions

The players stand in a loose circle and try to keep the ball in the air by patting it upwards. No one player can pat the ball more than once in a row and players *cannot* follow a pre-arranged order. The number of pats is counted until the ball hits a wall or drops to the floor. When this happens the group starts again, trying to beat the previous score.

Additions and variations

- Each time a player pats the ball they have to name a television programme. If a player cannot think of another programme they call out the previous programme name until a player comes up with a new name.
- The counting can be done individually or as a group.
- The game can be played with a science topic, e.g. players call out the names of the planets, or parts of the body, or the names of elements within the periodic table.

Tips

- If the group is large play the game in two or three groups and compare the scores.

Psst!

Can be used as a means to encourage listening in the group and to introduce a new topic and elicit responses and instigate discussion. Players have to pass a whispered statement around the circle from person to person and see if the original statement survives the journey or, if not, what message to emerges!

Instructions

Players sit in a circle and the leader whispers a sentence in the ear of the player on their right. This player then whispers what they heard into the ear of the player on their right. This continues around the circle until the whispered sentence has reached the player on the leader's left who then says out loud what they have just heard. The leader then says out loud the sentence they started the game with and the two are compared.

Tips

- The sentence can be a statement about the subject being studied and can thus provoke discussion.
- Players are only allowed to whisper the sentence they hear once and they have to pass on what they heard. The statement may be misheard but players must pass on what they hear and not what they think they should have heard.
- The exercise can also be used as a concluding exercise.

Touch three things

A useful way to warm the group up physically and to encourage listening, observation and concentration. Players have to touch the objects in the room named by the leader.

Instructions

Players stand in a circle, placing their right foot into the circle. Players take note of exactly where they are in the circle and which players they are standing next to. They will have to come back to this place in the circle. The leader calls out three items in the room (e.g. a door, a chair, a book) and then calls 'Go', at which point all the players leave the circle in order to touch these three items and then return to their position in the circle. Before moving on to the next three objects the leader can elicit information about the objects players touched (e.g. 'What is the chair made from?', 'Did the door feel cold?', etc).

Tips

- Encourage players to look out for each other, to play the game with urgency but no accidents! So long as there is more than one object in the room which fits the description the likelihood of collisions and/or bottlenecks can be reduced.
- The group can be divided into two or three groups (e.g. for three groups count to three repeatedly around the circle, all 'ones' are a group, all 'twos' another, etc.). Each group can be sent at a time to touch the objects while the remaining groups observe.
- Three is a good number to remember but you could play the game with an increased number of objects.
- This activity is a good way to get to know the space in which you are working and can be used to introduce a lab, where all the equipment is, and any health and safety issues.

Additions and variations

- The objects called out could be used to introduce a new topic.
- Instead of calling the names of objects, the leader could call out a description of the object, e.g. 'Something blue, something green and something yellow' or 'Something that feels hot, something that feels cold, something that feels warm'.
- The description can be more like a clue, e.g. 'Something made of wood, something made of metal, something made of plastic'.
- The last player back chooses the next three items to call out and so the game continues.

Two truths and one lie

To generate discussion about the topic and clarify what the group and individuals know about the subject. To engage players in the subject matter and to encourage listening and communication. Players have to share what they think is true and untrue about the topic.

Instructions

Put players into pairs and introduce the topic of the session. Allow the players a few moments on their own to think of two things they know to be true about the topic and one thing they know to be an untruth or a lie about the topic. The players then take it in turns to tell each other their two truths and one lie. They then each have to decide which statements their partner told them were true and which was a lie. Each pair then agrees on two of their truths and one of their lies to share with the rest of the group. The whole group has to agree which are the truths and which the lie.

Tips

- The same exercise can be used at the beginning of a topic and again at the end to compare knowledge and understanding of the topic.
- Players can be very obvious in their deception or be subtle and clever, and try to catch out their partner.

Additions and variations

- The same exercise can be played with a time limit in which players have to move around the room and tell as many people as possible the two truths and one lie. Players then feed back to the whole group any lies they heard and truths and also any statements of which they were unsure.

Appendix 2: optional student activities

This appendix contains the following optional student activity sheets

Microbes – the fight against disease (see page 10)

(To be used in conjunction with the material provided on the companion website. These suggested student activities are just for reference and versions to use or adapt can be downloaded from the companion website.)

 To remind pupils of the story of how Louis Pasteur noticed how hens treated with old cholera 'vaccine' survived a new dose of cholera, you can ask the pupils to rearrange cards showing episodes of the story provided on the www.scyd. co.uk website.

These questions could be used to help pupils focus on important elements of the story and the science concepts.

1. How can humans be infected with anthrax?
2. Why didn't the second set of healthy hens die when they were injected with the old cholera culture?
3. Why was Colin so against Pasteur's ideas about treating anthrax?
4. Why was Dubois prepared to pay money to set up the experiment with the sheep?
5. 25 untreated and 25 treated (injected with old anthrax cultures) sheep were injected with live anthrax. Why was this?
6. There were 60 sheep in all, so what happened to the other ten?
7. Do you think Pasteur was a brave or a rather arrogant scientist? Support your answer with evidence from the play script.

Food chains – energy transfer (see page 24)

1. How much water was in the bucket at the start of the 'food chain'?
2. (Make a table showing the results for each team.) How much water each team transferred?
3. Why did some teams transfer more water than others?
4. What might plants and animals at each level of the food chain be doing that would mean they need more or less energy to carry on with their lives?
5. What do the following parts of the game show that you might find in an ecosystem?
    a. The amount of water in the bucket at the start
    b. Student 1, Student 2, Student 3, Student 4
    c. The amount of water in the bucket at the end

Extended questions

1. What percentage of the original energy (water) in the bucket was transferred to the end of the food chain by each team?
2. How does this percentage amount of energy loss fit with what you know or can find out about energy lost at each level of an ecosystem?
3. Why must top predators (such as sharks, hawks, lions) take care about the amount of energy they need to hunt?

References

Adams, T. (2007). 'The new age of ignorance', *Observer Review*, 6, 1 July 2007.

Ainley, M. D. (1994). *Motivation and learning: psychology and you*. Victoria: Hawker Brownlow Education.

Alexander, P. A. (1997). 'Mapping the multidimensional nature of domain learning: The interplay of cognitive, motivational, and strategic forces'. In M. L. Maehr. and P. R.Pintrich (Eds), *Advances in motivation and achievement*. (213–50) Greenwich, Connecticut: JAI Press.

Bailey, S.D. (1993). *Wings to fly: Bringing theatre arts to students with special needs*.
Rockville, Maryland: Woodbine House.

Bergin, D.A. (1999). 'Influences on classroom interest'. *Educational Psychologist*, 34, (2) 87–98.

Butler, J. (1989). 'Science learning and drama processes'. *Science Education*, 73 (5), 569–79.

Cristofi, C. and Davis, M. (1991). 'Science through drama'. *Education in Science*, (141), 28–9.

Deci, E. L. (1992). 'The relation of interest to the motivation of behaviour: A self-determination of theory perspective'. In K.A. Renninger, S. Hidi and A. Krapp (Eds), *The role of interest in learning and development*. (pp. 43–71) Hillsdale, New Jersey: Lawrence Erlbaum Associates.

Dorion, K.R. (2009). 'Science through drama: A multiple case exploration of the characteristics of drama activities used in secondary science lessons'. *International Journal of Science Education*, 31(16), 2247–70.

Driver, R., Guesne, E. and Tiberghien, A. (Eds) (2000). *Children's ideas in science*. Milton Keynes: Open University Press.

Duveen, J. and Solomon, J. (1994). 'The great evolution trial: Use of role-play in the classroom'. *Journal of Research in Science Teaching*, 31 (5), 575–82.

Erickson, K. L. (1988). *Building castles in the classroom*. Language Arts, 65, 14–19.

Fels, L. and Meyer, K. (1997). 'On the edge of chaos: Co-evolving worlds of drama and science'. *Teaching Education*, 9(1), 75–81.

Gardner, H. (1983). *Frames of mind: The theory of multiple intelligences* (3rd Edition). Illinois: Skylight.

Gardner, H. (1991). *The unschooled mind: How children think and how schools should teach*. London: Fontana.

Herrmann, N. (1990). *The creative brain*. Lake Lure, North Carolina: Brain Books.

Kentish, B. (1995). 'Hypotheticals: deepening the understanding of environmental issues through ownership of learning'. *Australian Science Teachers Journal*. 41 (1), 21–5.

Langeveld, M.J. (1965). *In search of research. In Paedagogica Europoea: The European Year Book of Educational Research 1*. Amsterdam: Elsevier.

Levi, P. (2007). *The periodic table*. London: Penguin Classics.

McCaslin, N. (1996). *Creative drama in the classroom and beyond*. USA: Longman Publishers.

Medawar, P. (1984). *The limits of science*. Oxford: Oxford University Press.

Ogborn, J., Kress, G., Martins, I. and McGillicuddy, K. (1996). *Explaining science in the classroom*. Buckingham: Open University Press.

Renninger, K.A. (1998). 'The roles of individual interest(s) and gender in learning: An overview of research on preschool and elementary school-aged children/students.' In L. Hoffmann, A. Krapp, K. Renninger, and J. Baumert (Eds), *Interest and learning: Proceedings of the Seeon conference on interest and gender*. (165–75) Kiel, Germany: IPN.

Schiefele, U. (1996). 'Topic interest, text representation, and quality of experience'. *Contemporary Educational Psychology*, 12, 3–18.

Singsurf.org. 'Left brain, right brain, whole brain?' Article downloaded from www.singsurf.org. Acessed 5 November 2010.

Smilansky, S. (1968). *The effects of socio-dramatic play on disadvantaged preschool children*. New York: John Wiley.

Snow, C.P. (1993). *The two cultures*. Cambridge: Cambridge University Press.

Sperry, R. W. (1966). 'Brain bisection and consciousness'. In C. Eccles (Ed.) *How the self controls its brain*. New York: Springer-Verlag.

Stencel, J. and Barkoff, A. (1993). 'Protein synthesis: role-playing in the classroom'. *The American Biology Teacher*, 55 (2), 102–3.

Tytler, R (2007). *Re-imagining science education: Engaging students in science for Australia's future*. Camberwell, Victoria: Australian Council for Educational Research.

Wagner, B.J. (1979). *Dorothy Heathcote: Drama as a learning medium*. London: Hutchinson Education.

Webb, N. (1980). 'An analysis of group interaction and mathematical error in heterogeneous abilities groups'. *British Journal of Educational Psychology*, 50, 266–76.

White, R.T. (1979). 'Relevance of practical work to comprehension of physics'. *Physics Education*, 14, 384–87.

Notes on contributors

Ian Abrahams is a lecturer in Science Education in the Department of Education at the University of York, UK. His current research interests are in the areas of practical work, teachers' attitudes to science education, and the use of drama to teach science.

Ruth Amos is a lecturer in Science Education at the Institute of Education, University of London, UK. Her interests include the global dimension in science education and argumentation and decision-making in school science.

Martin Braund is Honorary Fellow at the University of York, UK, and Adjunct Professor in Education and Social Sciences at the Cape Peninsula University of Technology in Cape Town, South Africa. He has written books on teaching plant science, the outdoor classroom and transition.

Sandra Campbell is a lecturer in Science Education at the Institute of Education, University of London, UK. She currently uses drama and role play in the field of biology education as part of her work in Initial Teacher Education.

Erdem Erem has a BA in Primary Education from Hacettepe University, Turkey, and is a lecturer in Drama Education at Ege University, Turkey.

Bidi Iredale has a degree in drama and a Teaching Certificate in Secondary Education and is an actor and drama facilitator working in both theatre and education.

Chris Otter has a first degree in chemistry and an MA(Ed) and is subject coordinator for the science PGCE at the University of York, UK, and Director of Salters' Advanced Chemistry. Her interests include context-based curriculum development and the use of drama in school science.

Murat Sağlam has a PhD in Science Education from the University of York, UK. He is a Teacher Educator at Ege University in Turkey. Murat is particularly interested in developing the use of drama to teach science.

Rachael Sharpe has a BSc (Hons) in Educational Studies and Science and, having taught science in both primary and secondary schools, is currently studying for a PhD in Science Education at the University of York, UK.

Index